Elementary General Music

The Best of *MEJ*

Betty W. Atterbury, Editor

MUSIC EDUCATORS NATIONAL CONFERENCE

Book design by Karen M. Fields

Contents

LISTENING

MOVEMENT

CREATING

Section 4   To Share: Performance

Section 5   To Be Most Effective: Partnership

Introduction

by Betty W. Atterbury

One of the traditional purposes of the *Music Educators Journal (MEJ)* has been to serve as a forum for effective teaching approaches. In a recent survey, readers indicated that articles containing these practical suggestions are highly valued. The contents of this book are a sample of the many fine articles pertaining to elementary methodology that have been printed in the journal during the past twenty years. These articles were selected for reprint in this format because they offer unique and valuable classroom ideas not accessible elsewhere in a single source.

This selection of articles is designed both for the practicing teacher and the teacher-to-be. Because the contents were chosen from issues of the *MEJ* that date from 1970 on, younger teachers may have missed some of these ideas. Still other readers may have forgotten some of the teaching suggestions contained in one or many of these articles. Although our culture and the out-of-school backgrounds of students have changed somewhat during the past two decades, the music teaching techniques described in these articles have stood the test of time and continue to be worthwhile instructional ideas.

This collection of articles can also serve as a means of complementing and enhancing course content for students enrolled in undergraduate or graduate elementary methods courses. Some articles may reinforce a specific lecture or demonstration, whereas others may serve as a means of presenting a contrasting viewpoint. Methods teachers may wish to use one or more of the articles in this book and select additional articles from the *MEJ* or another music education publication to structure assignments that will provoke critical thinking and evaluation.

This book is not intended to serve as a methods textbook for undergraduates; rather, it is a set of effective "how-to" ideas. Because the selection is by one person, the contents reflect my beliefs about effective elementary general music teaching. It would not be practical to reprint all the worthwhile articles that have been published in *MEJ* on this topic. As is noted in the title, this collection is merely a sample of the best.

Betty W. Atterbury is associate professor of music education at the University of Southern Maine in Gorham.

Section

To Begin:
A Philosophical Framework

Elementary music teachers usually have an intensive work load. They often teach seven or more classes every day, and many teach in more than one building. Such a teaching schedule can intimidate the most musical and caring of human beings! To endure the pace and demands of teaching at this level, music educators must have a strong and cogent philosophical base. They must really know why they are teaching music.

One philosophical viewpoint that has many adherents in our profession is that espoused by Susanne Langer, Harry Broudy, Charles Leonhard, and Bennett Reimer. The music educators on this list have suggested that an ability to verbalize the nature and value of music is the logical philosophical underpinning for music education.

In the first article of this book, Sam Reese offers a clear and compelling discussion of this philosophical viewpoint. Reese describes how a secure philosophical understanding enables one to be a better music teacher.

How Do Your Ideas about Music Affect Your Teaching?

by Sam Reese

A bricklayer was building himself a home. Being pressed for time and concerned only with getting a particular wall to stand, he did not think much about how his home would look when the work was finished. Nor did he stop to inspect the ground on which his house would stand. Our misguided bricklayer simply set to work, concerned neither with the nature of the foundation for his home nor with his end product. He thought only about his immediate concern, unmindful of his ultimate end.

As might be expected, the bricklayer unhappily encountered many problems. As he erected the other walls to his house, he found that they would not meet squarely at the corners. Soon the walls began to sink into the ground, since they were standing on a weak foundation. Obviously, the home was never lived in.

Establishing Foundations

It is easy to recognize this bricklayer's mistakes, but before we point a condemning finger, we should ask ourselves if we as music teachers are not in a similar position. Like the bricklayer, we have often failed to consider the foundations on which we are

Sam Reese is Director of Fine Arts and Technology in the Community Consolidated School District #64, Park Ridge, Illinois. This article originally appeared in the February 1976 Music Educators Journal.

building our music structure. We have not adequately developed a solid understanding of the nature and the value of music. In our hurried involvement with everyday teaching, we have frequently failed to do the proper amount of speculation to ensure that our walls will match up. Without a clear idea of what the goals of our teaching are, we have become so engrossed with our means (everyday activities) that they are actually incompatible with our educational ends.

At the root of this problem are a general lack of critical thought by music educators about the problems of aesthetics and a lack of awareness of how aesthetic problems affect educational practice. An understanding of aesthetics—the philosophical inquiry that seeks to answer questions about the nature of music and its value for human life—is needed by every music educator.

Asking ourselves "What is the nature of music?" brings many different answers. Music is sound used for self-expression; music is rhythm, melody, harmony; music is the combination of tones; music is organized sound; music is any sound intended to be music. A similar range of responses results from asking "What is the value of music for human life?" Music is valuable as a leisure-time activity; music is valuable for purging emotions; music is valuable as a challenging, intellectual endeavor; music offers valuable insights into the nature of human feelings. An adherence to one or more of these views of the nature and value of music will affect the way music is taught—which aspects are emphasized, which characteristics are considered less valuable, and which type of approach is taken. If confronted with these two questions, most of us would feel hard-pressed to give answers that reach deeper than the much-simplified standard responses I have mentioned. Yet the consideration of these questions is the foundation on which all of music education stands. If we cannot give clear, intelligent answers to these questions, we cannot hope to justify our existence in public education nor even satisfactorily answer for ourselves why we personally have devoted our efforts to presenting music to children.

What Are We *Really* Teaching?

Perhaps it is not clear how our understanding of the nature and value of music affects classroom practice. A few practical illustrations may help.

Consider a teacher who spends a great deal of instructional time simply singing songs with children. Little investigation of the music material presented in the songs takes place. Just one song after another is sung. Whether the teacher realizes it or not, these classroom activities present a fairly clear opinion about the nature of music. According to this teacher, music is simply sound to be enjoyed. Apparently, little discourse is needed to bring about this enjoyment. Music should just be as pleasurable and as much fun as possible. Also, according to this teacher's actions, music is valuable because it provides us with enjoyment and relaxation. Serious involvement and rich, significant experiences are apparently subordinate to more immediately satisfying contacts with music. This teacher has obviously not devoted much time to an investigation of the nature of music and its significant value for human life. Consequently, her students probably will learn to hold similar ideas about music and may not value music as a source of life-enriching experience.

Let us examine how another teacher's aesthetic theories (conscious or not) affect classroom practice. Recordings of program music constitute a major portion of this teacher's instructional materials. Considerable time is devoted to program read-ing, with attention directed to the music techniques used to tell the story. ("Hear how the flute sounds like a bird.") Also, when a song is sung, an investigation of the meaning or "message" of the lyric is conducted. Any analysis of music elements is of secondary importance. The teacher makes it a point to sing songs with the "proper messages" for elementary children and is currently making an effort to be "relevant" by singing songs about pollution, world peace, and the dangers of drugs. According to this teacher, this programmatic music literature is the type most appropriate for children, since he believes that their understanding is too unsophisticated for "formal, abstract" music that lacks a story or a message. The primary function of music, then, is to tell stories or carry messages. When music refers us to something—a story, an idea, or an emotion—it is fulfilling its true nature. This teacher believes that the value of music is its ability to inform or teach us about aspects of life in an interesting and pleasant manner. He is practicing what is often called referentialist aesthetic theory. As an outcome of this type of instruction, students value almost all popular music (since it has words) and any "serious" music that tells a story. Any other music does not seem to fit their idea of what music should be.

Consider yet another aesthetic position, traditionally known as formalism, as manifested in classroom practice. This teacher believes that the most valuable aspects of music are those formal elements that can be objectively agreed upon. Almost all instructional time is spent analyzing and identifying these elements. Whenever a song is sung or a composition listened to, an extensive analysis is undertaken. The meter, modality, harmonic style, prominent rhythm patterns, prominent melodic patterns and themes, and type of formal construction are all identified and discussed. This teacher does not mention expressive qualities, feelings, emotions, or any extramusical aspect that might be presented by the music, nor does he allow his students to discuss these experiences in class, believing that these aspects of music experience are too "subjective." Music is to be apprehended with the intellect. Consequently, when these students listen to music, they do their best to identify formal elements and "analyze" the composition on the spot. The listener who can identify the greatest number of formal elements, it is believed, has had the fullest music experience. For this teacher, and thus for his students, the essential nature of music is its complex combination of formal properties of sound. Music is a complex puzzle to be figured out. The value of music for human life stems from the exciting intellectual challenge presented to the human mind.

A still different aesthetic position, sometimes known as absolute expressionism, is held by the teacher in this last example. This teacher believes that it is of the utmost importance that the music material used in her classroom be genuinely expressive. She is concerned that the music be "good" music and that it be capable of calling forth a feelingful response from her students. A typical lesson might proceed something like this: First, the music is presented to the class (the recording is played or the song is sung) from beginning to end so that the children can experience it. The next step involves pointing out the musical elements that are responsible for the peculiar affective aesthetic effect presented by the music. In this way, the experience of the music becomes refined and enriched. The melodic shape is analyzed, the meter is identified, important rhythm patterns are pointed out, dynamic changes are investigated, and whatever else is musically significant is discovered. But the teacher does not stop here. The music is presented again in its entirety for experiencing by the students now that they have had a chance to perceive more accurately what is contained in the music. The most important factors in music experience for this teacher are sensitive perception of the music elements and affective reaction to these elements. Through lessons of this sort, the teacher attempts to systematically develop her students' ability to perceive and also provides ample opportunity for them to feel (experience, react to) what the music makes them feel. In her classroom, nonverbal music experience receives top priority, with music study being an aid to this experience. According to this teacher, the essential nature of music is its ability to provide rich, significant, feelingful experience completely through its aesthetic elements—that is, without referring to something outside the music. The value of music for human life is its ability to present and explore unique human feeling and thus provide insights into human subjective reality.[1]

Aesthetics Are for Everyone

I hope it is clearer now how beliefs about the nature and value of music (aesthetic theories) actually do influence classroom practice. Although the illustrations may seem a bit naive in that they show teachers as being "black or white," unchanging and rigid in their approaches, we can all recognize a bit of ourselves in each of these situations. We can see from these examples that aesthetic inquiry is not merely an abstract process carried on by college professors, but is something that should concern every music teacher.

Unless the music teacher has relatively clear and well-founded beliefs about the nature and value of music, it may be presented in a manner contrary to its real nature. Relatively trivial aspects of music may receive undue emphasis, while more significant characteristics may be overlooked. The reading of notation, the development of performance skill, the ability to identify formal elements, or the memorization of technical terms may become ends in themselves, when in reality they are merely means that help develop the true end, which is aesthetic sensitivity. These activities are not valuable in themselves, but only insofar as they contribute to the ability to respond deeply and fully to experiences with music. However, without devoting some effort to aesthetic inquiry, a teacher may not realize that he or she is neglecting the aspect of music that is most valuable for human life.

The starting point for developing goals, objectives, and specific activities for a music program should be the articulation of the nature and value of music. This set of beliefs would establish the direction of our instruction. It would stipulate the purpose for teaching music and delineate what students are to gain from this instruction. These beliefs would become the "target" of our efforts.

Too often, under the pressure of heavy schedules, the development of specific classroom activities precedes any careful thought about what is to be gained from the experience or how it will contribute to overall sensitivity to music. When the end goal of instruction is not clear, an inconsistency of action is likely to result. Music might easily be presented first in one way, then another—each way incompatible with the other. Students are bound to come away confused, wondering just what music is supposed to do and how it really should be experienced. Bennett Reimer has said,

> It is almost unheard-of for a course of study to be aesthetically consistent. Since most teachers are not aware of the disparate aesthetic positions exemplified by their activities, they are not aware that their activities are very often in opposition, producing results which are aesthetically incompatible. [2]

Valuing Our Work

The goal of instruction should become the standard by which we judge the value of our specific activities. If we are unsure of the worth of a certain activity, we will be able to judge it by how significantly it contributes to the reaching of our end goal. For example, we can determine the relative merits of teaching notation skills, performance skills, various concepts, and so on, and how much time and emphasis should be placed on these activities by deciding whether they actually enhance the ability to experience (perceive and react to) music in a significant way. Activities that do not contribute to this goal should be given little or no instructional time. We cannot possibly judge the value of our objectives and activities if we do not understand the nature of music and the reasons for teaching it.

Having a clear idea of the nature of music and its value not only improves the outcomes achieved by students involved in the instructional process; it also can provide teachers with an understanding of the value of their work. It can give our work that sense of meaning and purpose that is essential if the teaching is to be of high quality. Teachers, who all too frequently work under very frustrating conditions, need to believe that their work is of high value. As they walk into the classroom day after day, they need to know that their actions are contributing significantly to the improvement of human life. If the profession in general and teachers as individuals are to maintain vital and lively attitudes, we must have a clear idea of why we are investing so much effort in teaching music to children. We cannot continue the difficult job of teaching if we believe that we are merely teaching children how to sight-sing or to identify duple meter or to count rhythms with a 3/4 meter signature. We must have larger goals and ideals to guide us. We need to understand the value of music for human life and the ways it can ultimately improve the quality of our civilization. Our jobs can quickly become mundane and insignificant without an ideal to set our sights on.

As teachers of music, then, we must ask ourselves two very basic questions: "What is music?" and "What is the value of music for human life?" If these questions seem difficult—and for most of us they certainly do—we need to spend some time reading and thinking about the field of aesthetics. [3] Of course, for teachers who are already burdened with professional work, it is no simple task to find the time to read. On the other hand, too many music teachers limit their concerns to completely practical matters. They assume the attitude that "If it doesn't tell me how to teach class on Tuesday, I'm not interested." These are the teachers who are likely to present contrasting and incompatible views about music to their students, and who are prone to tire quickly of the sameness of teaching day after day. Therefore, do not assume that the answers to these questions have no effect on our practical teaching activities. Theory and practice are not unrelated, but exist in a dialectical relationship. We all have certain beliefs about the nature and value of music. Why not invest some time and effort in aesthetic inquiry to ensure that our ideas are clear and are built on strong foundations? This investment may make you a more forceful and a more inspired teacher.

Notes

1. See Bennett Reimer, *A Philosophy of Music Education* (Englewood Cliffs, NJ: Prentice-Hall, 1970) for a full explanation of this aesthetic position.

2. Bennett Reimer, *Development and Trial in a Junior and Senior High School of a Two-Year Curriculum in General Music* (Washington, DC: U.S. Department of Health, Education, and Welfare, Office of Education, Bureau of Research, 1967), p. 37.

3. The following books provide a helpful introduction to the fields of aesthetics and aesthetic education: Harry S. Broudy, *Enlightened Cherishing: An Essay on Aesthetic Education* (Urbana: University of Illinois Press, 1972). John Dewey, *Art As Experience* (New York: Capricorn Books, 1958). Susanne K. Langer, *Feeling and Form: A Philosopher's Theory of Art* (New York: Charles Scribner's Sons, 1953); *Philosophy in a New Key: A Study in the Symbolism of Reason, Rite, and Art*, 3d ed. (Cambridge, MA: Harvard University Press, 1957); and *Problems of Art: Ten Philosophical Lectures* (New York: Charles Scribner's Sons, 1957). Leonard B. Meyer, *Emotion and Meaning in Music* (Chicago: University of Chicago Press, 1956). Bennett Reimer, ed., *Toward an Aesthetic Education* (Washington, DC: Music Educators National Conference, 1971).

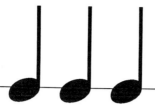

Section

To Endure: Classroom Management

One of the most important aspects of elementary music teaching is not related to the extensive musical background that prospective teachers receive in their undergraduate education. There are a number of specific skills required in order to be a successful elementary music teacher. All of these skills are subsumed in a single term used in teaching—the word "discipline." It is the ability to "discipline," or the "lack of discipline," that can make or break a teacher.

The authors of the four articles in this section each describe important aspects of discipline (classroom management) that contribute to competent teaching. Fairness, consistency, teacher image and presence, and the importance of sharing the lesson agenda with each class are strategies described in the initial article.

Classroom management is also affected by lesson pacing, a concept that prospective teachers often have difficulty understanding. Although some teachers believe this facet of teaching to be intuitive, the author of the second article believes that the specific aspects of effective pacing can be verbalized. All music teachers can, indeed, become masters at correctly pacing a lesson.

Each elementary music teacher meets hundreds of students each week, and knowing each child's name is an enormously important part of effective classroom control. The third article describes a variety of music activities incorporating children's names. Using these suggestions, especially at the beginning of the school year, will enable teachers to quickly succeed in this important aspect of classroom discipline.

Teacher organization also has an important impact on classroom management. The final article in this section includes effective ideas for all teachers. These suggestions range from knowing who has had a turn playing the Vibraslap to preparing for substitute teachers.

Guidelines on Classroom Management for Beginning Music Educators

by Margaret Dee Merrion

"Are the kids like this all of the time?" asks a junior practicum student in disbelief.

"How do you get the class to listen?" asks a senior starting her student teaching.

"How can I maintain better discipline?" worries another student teacher at midterm.

"I'm not sure I want to teach!"

As a supervising teacher of music, I have had such questions posed and thoughts shared with me on countless occasions by students in our college of education who undergo three phases of practicum experiences. Phase one and two experiences entail a number of hours of classroom observation, tutoring, and small- and large-group teaching in preparation for phase three—student teaching. These future teachers essentially share one major concern—classroom discipline, now more

Margaret Dee Merrion is dean of the College of Fine Arts at Ball State University, Muncie, Indiana. At the time she wrote this article, she was an assistant professor of teaching at the University of Northern Iowa, Cedar Falls, where she taught at the university's Malcolm Price Laboratory School. Merrion has written articles and books on music education and served as the guest editor of the special focus section on "Research in the Music Classroom" in the November 1990 Music Educators Journal. This article originally appeared in the February 1980 Music Educators Journal.

fashionably termed "classroom management." It is not surprising that this concern is also the number one dissatisfaction among many parents of schoolchildren.

It seems to me that our teacher-training institutions are more competent than ever in instilling the basics of educational psychology. Practicum students have no difficulty understanding reinforcement schedules, theories of motivation, concept formation, and even behavior modification. Furthermore, music education students are often fairly well skilled in music reading and performing skills. The instructional management phase of teaching thus offers little threat to most beginning teachers. The most frightening of all first-day jitters remains the task of classroom management.

Fortunately or unfortunately, the issue of classroom management in music instruction poses unique problems due to the aesthetic nature of the arts. To maintain a learning environment free enough to permit personal and individual responses, improvisation, and creativity while providing a structure in which all students can collectively remain on-task and actively involved seems impossible. Just how *does* one manage classroom behavior?

Preventive Discipline

I would like to propose a few preventive discipline measures. They are by no means the most essential strategies, but rather a few techniques especially applicable to music educators. No discipline strategy can compare with the sense of credibility teachers must establish once they are on the job. Of paramount importance is one's genuine interest in and respect for children. There are, however, a number of factors the teacher can directly prepare for and control through advance planning.

No discipline strategy can compare with the sense of credibility teachers must establish once they are on the job. Of paramount importance is one's genuine interest in and respect for children. There are, however, a number of factors the teacher can directly prepare for and control through advance planning.

Even though the times may change, certain classroom management practices should remain constant. Two of these policies are fairness and consistency. When fairness and consistency prevail, a certain sense of security exists within the classroom. Fairness also builds trust, the foundation of any good relationship. A child's perception of a teacher's authority rests on the fairness and consistency with which the teacher manages. Children then have a better understanding of what behaviors are appropriate and what measures will be taken should behaviors deviate.

A gentle and sensitive teacher I encountered during my student-teaching period offered a third procedure for preventive discipline: "Come into the classroom with an iron fist; later, you will find you can put on a velvet glove." In this era of permissiveness, I find few who advocate such apparently strict firmness, but this advice does not relate to corporal punishment or "never smile before Christmas" practices. Rather, it is meant to address the attitude a teacher conveys. The expectations that an educator sets as appropriate classroom behavior must be the highest at the beginning of the school year. If the expectations are low

or even mediocre, students will merely conform to those second-rate levels. Another important consideration for music educators is that they generally teach a child for more than one school year. It is therefore crucial to begin the school year with a structured, well-conceived management plan that can operate throughout the school year as well as the ensuing years.

We know that three types of learning are operative at all times: cognitive, motor-skill, and affective. In music education, teachers must be committed to the priority of the affective goal and never short-change that aim. Regardless of the type of learning experiences, students and teachers of music must not compromise any aesthetic end for a cognitive or motor-skill learning. This fourth aspect of preventive discipline is of central importance.

I recently observed a high school choral director spend close to an hour rehearsing several opening measures of one selection from a musical. The precision with which the students sharpened their dramatic and musical skills in that single rehearsal was a remarkable indication that exceptional educational success can be achieved in performing-oriented experiences. The personal and collective rewards were not necessarily on opening night of the musical, but during these moments when each member of the group began to know and feel the proper vocal balance and gestures.

Because music educators often spend the majority of their instructional hours in process, it is in their favor that aesthetic rewards be realized in the process of learning fine music literature and not just in the final product of public performance. Selecting music experiences capable of strong and rewarding aesthetic outcomes not only ensures on-task behaviors but eliminates distractive and disruptive behaviors by virtue of involvement.

Teacher Presence

A fifth preventive discipline measure has to do with a teacher's physical image. The saying "never judge a book by its cover" is a lesson one *learns*; one's natural inclination is to judge a book, person, or place by its outward appearance. My observations of elementary schoolchildren reinforce this suspicion: Books and materials often are selected by children for their visually attractive colors, drawings, sizes, or shapes. Similarly, children also may judge teachers by their physical appearance.

Recent research discussed in *The Master Teacher* indicated that not only the style but even the color of clothing has a direct effect on children.[1] Although it is not possible to compile lists of what a teacher should or should not wear in the classroom, one can confidently assure practicing teachers that T-shirts and jeans only reinforce an overly casual relationship with children. Ask yourself: If you were seated in a room with a number of other adults, would a child approach you for information, suspecting you were a teacher by your dress?

The matter of image and presence is not easy to document. Yet numerous administrators instinctively search out this trait during the hiring process. It is a characteristic that often indicates competence and ability to manage learning and behavior. Children meet teachers visually before they meet them aurally. The ever-so-slight advantage of sight before sound can help or hinder the establishment of respect.

Other facets of teacher presence include the pitch and tempo of one's speaking voice (when instructing, when disciplining, or when talking on a one-to-one basis); facial expressions of approval and disapproval; teaching postures; and frequency of posture changes. These behaviors need forethought and practice before actual teaching contact. Decide how long you will remain seated at the piano; experiment with your facial expressions in the mirror; and record your voice and check it for clarity, sincerity, and direction.

The effectiveness of these aspects of teacher presence, of course, depends upon two conditions. The first is the degree of their compatibility within the teacher's personality. A second consideration is the nature of one's student clientele, including the size of the group and the ages, learning styles, abilities, and disabilities of the children.

Sharing Agendas

A final effective strategy I have used in general music is what I call "sharing the agenda." Because the general music class provides opportunities for children to engage in a diverse variety of activities, students often can come into the classroom curious, anxious, and even overmotivated. One key to effective management of these energies is to share the agenda for that period with the children as soon as they arrive.

Recently, my five-year-old daughter accompanied me on a number of errands with the understanding that there would be a long-awaited stop for ice cream. I explained to her that our agenda would include a number of stops. First we needed to stop at the dry cleaners, then walk to the post office. Next we would drive to the drug store, go on to the ice-cream shop, and finally stop at the gas station. I found that this method of sharing the agenda was quite helpful in organizing and directing our errands, especially if we were delayed by traffic. My daughter was assured we would proceed to each destination regardless of minor interruptions. Knowing the plan facilitated the flow of events.

Similarly, if a music teacher has only four Autoharps and twenty-four students who each want to perform a solo, sharing the agenda can assist in managing behavior throughout the class period. Each child is secure in the expectation of his or her eventual turn on the Autoharp.

Sharing agendas also serves as a cognitive framework for music experiences. For example, in teaching the concept of melodic direction, one might open the class period by explaining that the plan will include discussion, singing songs with different melodic directions, playing directions on bells, listening for direction of melodies on recordings, moving in different directions, and reading melodies of various directions. One might begin with the children giving directions for getting to the library from the classroom. Following that discussion, the children can explore road signs that give directions. After they have convinced the teacher that they know what "direction" is, it is the teacher's turn on the agenda to tell what he or she knows about direction. When children understand that the teaching/learning process relies on two-way communication, they are more responsive to listening when it is their turn.

A student teacher under my supervision once had an uncomfortable delay in finding a particular piano selection in a large anthology. Her annoyance with herself was pleasantly counteracted by the patient and cooperative spirit of the students, who obviously realized that she was organized but momentarily delayed in facilitating the next learning experience. It clearly was not a let-me-see—what-shall-we-do-next pause. Children who are not sure of the conceptual and behavioral bearings of a music class may misconstrue such delays. Often they will use that time for undesirable classroom behaviors.

In music methods courses I have taught, I always have required students to demonstrate and teach or peer-teach a segment of a lesson. Even though college students serve as an unrealistic learning audience, the skill of conceiving a lesson plan and executing it with a comfortable pace and flow is an attainable goal within an artificial setting. It is my hope that once student teachers are in their practicum experiences, their instructional skills will be secure, and time then can be appropriated for classroom management.

Much of the art and many of the skills of effective teaching can be learned in a variety of settings. Some students are able to learn vicariously via astute observation. Other may sharpen their skills in parenting. If one is committed to the joyous and rewarding ends of music education, each learning experience must be facilitated effectively. Few of us would question the necessity of instructional planning (lesson plans, advance selection and study of repertory, organization of learning outcomes). With classroom behavior management, similar preventive planning can reduce the anxiety and probability of disenchanting experiences while enhancing the positiveness of effective teaching and learning.

Note

1. Robert L. DeBruyn, "Dress for Respect," *The Master Teacher*, vol. 9, no. 9 (November 19, 1978), p. 1.

Pacing: The Tempo of Teaching

by Ann Small

"Sing with your head voice." "Follow the line of the phrase." "Try to improve your ear." These directions may be clearer to teachers who speak them than to learners who hear them. Well-worn phrases have little practical meaning in the classroom if they are not specifically defined. Unfortunately, students do not always know that they do not understand. Communication barriers increase when a learner is unaware of a problem and does not ask for an explanation.

"Pacing" is a term that student teachers in a music methods class may often hear but not understand. Pacing is discussed, practiced, even evaluated, but seldom defined. College students assume that, they should know what pacing means and, therefore, are afraid to ask for a clear definition. Pacing can be defined through action, so it can be measured and can lead to skill in capturing and holding students' interest.

At the outset, it is important to acknowledge that just as pacing cannot replace methods, methods cannot compensate for poor pacing. Because experience does not guarantee expertise, it is necessary to examine closely this essential but elusive element of effective teaching.

Ann Small is a professor of music education at Stetson University, DeLand, Florida. This article originally appeared in the May 1979 Music Educators Journal *under the title of "Pace Yourself."*

What Is Pacing?

Pacing is the act of moving through each activity in a lesson plan in addition to the transition periods between activities. Important to an understanding of pacing are its visible or audible results, which are observable in the behavior of students.

Effective pacing occurs when the teacher maintains a tempo appropriate for the age and interest level of the learners. It is possible for a teacher to plan entertaining events in a lesson and move through those events with lightning speed while students sit and watch. The teacher may assume that the lesson was successful just because it moved quickly. The actual result, however, is an exhausted teacher and students who may have participated in the same way that a spectator witnesses a sports event.

When studying pacing, teachers should observe and measure student responses as defined by their reactions. Specific learning behaviors such as hand-raising, moving, and performing can indicate attentiveness and might be considered results of appropriate pacing. Fidgeting, gazing into space, or whispering may be overt indications that the rate of events is too slow. Shouting, banging instruments, and hopping up and down may result from frantic pacing. It is true that undesirable actions also may occur from a lack of discipline, so the ability to identify cause-effect relationships is obviously important. Experienced teachers, however, will agree that inappropriate pacing will cause or contribute to discipline problems, even when lesson plans are musically impeccable.

Defining the acts and results of pacing necessitates pinpointing both what the teacher does and what the students do in response. What do teachers do when pacing? Teachers use their voices. The speed of speech and the pitch and loudness of the voice affect teaching momentum because they evoke emotional responses. The use of a tape recorder is an excellent way to evaluate vocal and speech patterns. Teachers can convey enthusiasm when pacing by raising their eyebrows, smiling, and modeling participation through singing, listening, and playing. All of these actions are overt behaviors.

Teachers can move from one area of the room to another, and the quickness of that movement can be observed in time intervals. Teachers can encourage student-teacher interaction by naming or touching individuals; such specific instances can be seen or heard and counted.

Other pacing actions include using eye contact, conducting, verbally starting or stopping activities, and cuing. All behaviors affect the tempo of a lesson.

Improving Pacing Skills

Time the details. Since pacing is performing in time, it would be beneficial for the teacher to become more temporally aware of his or her current pacing. A good place to start may be to measure the actual time one usually spends on activities that are considered necessary but are nonmusical, such as giving verbal instruction, walking from one place in the room to another, or writing on the chalkboard. A surprising amount of lesson time that is spent on nonmusic mechanics might be eliminated in the interest of more time for music. For instance, if children always go to the same room for music, a teacher can save a few seconds by placing a chosen record on the turntable before the lesson. The music part of a music class lasts longer when instructional charts have been positioned and selected materials and instruments have been placed around the room prior to starting time. Even teachers who travel from room to room can find ways to eliminate so-called essentials during lesson time.

Plan the length of activities. Implementing a variety of activities that focus on a single lesson objective is a productive teaching technique. The flow of activities is enhanced when the teacher allots a specific time limit to each event and then generally adheres to it when moving through the lesson plan. Such a schedule prevents stalling on one or two activities and promotes wider exposure to music experiences for the students.

Start with music. Music at a lesson's outset can spark interest, whereas talking can stifle it. Although a guide to listening may be necessary, it need not always be spoken. A teacher can elicit certain responses through facial expressions or body movements after the music has begun. Necessary brief verbalization always can precede a second hearing. Rhythm activities and question-answer games are also motivating openers, and pacing is improved when these activities are conducted with gestures instead of explanations.

Keep the group involved. Performance in the general music classroom is often enhanced by individual or group parts that require close teacher attention. Students who are anxious to make music, however, may not be willing to wait while individuals or isolated groups receive separate instruction on a part. Uninvolved students will quickly get bored or restless when they perceive a gap in pacing. Creative teachers can avoid these problem lags by initiating different unison activities and then using signals to conduct group divisions. Students can imitate on cue, so an individual or group can learn a new part while other performers sing or play. Some educators choose to teach all parts to all students and then conduct divisions and cue part entrances as the activity proceeds. As a result, instruction takes the form of music, everyone participates, and the temporal flow of the lesson is not interrupted.

Move around the room. The atmosphere of a lesson can assume the character of motion when the teacher actually moves around the room during the music period. Staying in the same place creates predictability that is conducive to boredom, which can soon turn into misbehavior. Teaching from the back, side, middle, and front of the classroom varies the focus of attention if activities are teacher-directed. When the teacher moves, the pace of the lesson moves. Touching students as one moves around the room also promotes an atmosphere of motion. Since touching produces a physical sensation, it usually engages the student's attention. Students who have been momentarily distracted can be drawn back to the lesson, and seconds that would have elapsed during a verbal reprimand can be spent on continuous music learning.

It is possible for a teacher to plan entertaining events in a lesson and move through those events with a lightning speed while students sit and watch. The teacher may assume that the lesson was successful just because it moved quickly.

Sometimes, however, teachers can waste time in walking. For example, if the plan calls for singing followed by guided listening to a recording, empty time can occur as the teacher walks to the record player. The combination of waiting until the end of the song to start to walk, getting the record ready, and fumbling for the correct band can create an awkward time lag. Even if the record has been placed on the turntable prior to the lesson, valuable time will be lost in a walk used only for traveling.

An effective alternative exists. The record can be placed before starting time, and, as the singing activity is concluded, the walk to the record player can begin. With one hand, the teacher can conduct the final cutoff and with the other immediately place the needle on the previously identified band. The time spent in changing locations will then be time also spent in teaching music.

Disguise transitions. A variety of focused activities tends to improve lesson pacing, but potential for momentum lag between lesson events increases. Teachers who carefully organize plans and materials occasionally may be unaware of time gaps that are created by statements such as "Now we are going to sing..." and "Turn to page..." followed by brief pauses. Instructions for a group to leave their desks and assemble on the rug, followed by a period of silence during which the children move, also can cause pacing to stall. To the imaginative child, these moments of nothingness can signal an opportunity to create alternatives to participation, such as clowning, shoving, scaring the fish in the aquarium, or hiding under the table.

To eliminate these pacing interruptions, a teacher should carefully plan the actual process of changing activities. Transitions can be creatively disguised so that students do not sense independent happenings, all having a beginning and ending. Singing, pantomiming, conducting, and moving can hide transitions—even those that include instructions. Indicating directions to the group through facial expressions, movement, head nods, or other gestures may accomplish a needed change without verbal instructions followed by a pause. As a result, lessons will gain continuity and maintain momentum. Music events will seem to overlap, and students will sense fewer opportunities for disruption.

Music educators have every advantage for success in the classroom. Colorful materials, fun songs, learning games, audiovisual aids, and methods books are readily available. The skill of teaching music, however, is not for sale. Proficiency in the classroom includes temporal awareness, the ability to manipulate techniques in time, and identification and rehearsal of specific pacing actions. Learners tune in when music speaks if teachers maintain an appropriate tempo of teaching.

Name Games

by Linda K. Damer

Learning the name of each child in your music class is important but often difficult, especially for the elementary general music teacher who travels to several schools and teaches nine or ten classes per day. Discipline problems often can be averted by speaking the child's name, without breaking the concentration of the class on the music task at hand. Many have experienced this dialogue:

"You, stop punching the girl next to you."

"Who? Me?"

"Yes, you, in the red-striped shirt..." and the class concentration is lost. A simple "George" interjected into the teacher's presentation might have been sufficient to stop the undesired behavior.

Teachers impart to the child a feeling of self-worth when they call the child by name, both in the classroom and in the halls. Music teachers can develop music activities that encourage the child to respond to his or her name. These activities may be especially useful in teaching mentally handicapped students to recognize their names.

Even if teachers are established "fixtures" in a school system and know all of the children's names through nurturing them from kindergarten on, their student teachers, who spend such a brief time in music classrooms, can be more effective if they learn the children's names. The following activities, all centering on the child's name, may help the music teacher learn the children's names as the students participate in educational music activities. Each of these suggestions can be incorporated into the regular music curriculum and can be used for a short time at the beginning of the music class period or as a concluding activity in time remaining at the end of the period.

For instance, a name tag for each child can be a source of many different music activities, all of which will help teachers learn children's names. Making the name tags at the opening of the school year is time-consuming, but the music return is worth it. The name tag should be made from substantial, paper-like tagboard, and the printing should be large enough to be read from the back of the room. Many school systems provide laminating services or have a laminating machine available; if not, clear contact paper can be applied to the front surface of the tag. Because tagboard comes in large pieces, it will save time to print the names on it while it is still in one large piece, using a yardstick to help keep the divisions. Then laminate the large sheet or apply the contact paper, and finally cut it into individual name tags on a paper cutter.

Names and Notes

For the primary grades, especially kindergarten to second grade, write only the child's first name on the tag. Then choose a music symbol for the class to learn, and draw it on the tags. For ex-

Linda K. Damer is a professor of music at Indiana State University in Terre Haute. This article originally appeared in the March 1981 Music Educators Journal and was reprinted in the journal in February 1991.

ample, first graders should learn to recognize whole, half, quarter, and eighth notes and be able to move in rhythm to them. Divide the class into four groups, and put a different note on each group's name tag. Color-key the tags by making all the whole notes red, half notes blue, quarter notes green, and eighth notes brown. Prepare four large signs to place on the walls around the room, one for each note with its name written with the symbol. Again, the signs can be color-keyed to follow the theme.

Many music activities relate to this idea. Students can find someone else in the class who has a note like theirs. This can be done as a chain activity; one child finds a classmate who has a matching note, and the new child finds another student with the same. The chain continues until all children with matching notes have joined. While holding up one of the large signs, ask all who have that kind of note on their tags to stand up. Teachers can also point to each note and ask that all children who have it stand by the sign. A fourth activity is to ask the whole class to walk silently around the room to find the sign that matches their name tags.

When the children are ready, teachers should introduce the names of the notes. Each child will learn the notes by name both aurally and visually. As the children's development permits, they can put body rhythms to their notes. For example, the whole-note group can tap a foot on one to a count of four. The half-note group can snap the fingers on one and three, and quarter notes can *patsch* on every beat. Eighth notes can clap the eight beats. The children will eventually be able to combine rhythms: two against each other, then three, and finally all four. Throughout all of these activities the child's name is there for teachers to learn. Other symbols, such as rests, treble clef, bass clef, sharps, flats, natural signs, or pictures of instruments, are suitable for use on the tags.

Names and Rhythms

Another type of music activity that incorporates the use of name tags uses the rhythm of the child's name. The level of the activity can be geared to the abilities of the group. As the class sits in a circle, the teacher can go around the circle saying and clapping names, asking each child how many claps were in his or her name. Then the children can say and clap their own names. When they have understood this concept, choose two students to stand in front of the class, and let the class clap the rhythm of the two names together. When students can easily do this, try four names (see figure 1).

Variations of this activity include each child playing the rhythm of his or her name on a rhythm instrument or on a pitched bar instrument with only C, E, and G on it. A different sound could be used for each child's name, with the class repeating the rhythms presented by the four children.

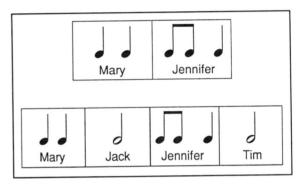

Figure 1. Clapping activity

As another activity, four or eight names can be incorporated into a rhyme. For kindergarten and first grade, only four names each time are appropriate, and the activity should be planned for later in the year.

> *Arlie, Heather, D.J., Drew*
> *Got their shoes stuck in the glue.*
> *Nancy, Jennifer, Brian, Lee*
> *All were stung by a buzzing bee.*

Although this activity doesn't use the students' name tags except for bookkeeping purposes, it will help teachers learn the children's names and will again focus on individuals. The class can read the rhyme together and then clap the rhythm as they read the words. The four (or eight) students can each come to the front of the class and choose a sound for his or her name. It can be charted for the class to follow (see figure 2).

Figure 2. Class rhyme

The four students are the "soloists," and each does the sound for his or her name; the class is the "orchestra" and does the sounds for the rest of the rhyme. Do it first with spoken words and sounds; then eliminate audible words as the children continue with the motions.

Names and Variations

As another variation of this activity, let each of the four students choose a rhythm instrument with which to play his or her name. The soloists play the rhythm of their names, and the class uses sounds for the rest of the rhyme—again speaking the rhyme aloud and then thinking the rhyme as they play (see figure 3).

Figure 3. Class rhyme with instruments

A third variation adds the concept of dynamics. Mark one line piano, the second forte, third pianissimo, and fourth fortissimo to see if students can make the contrasting dynamic levels with their voices. The concepts of crescendo and decrescendo can also be introduced in this manner. Expression in the voice can be emphasized for another variation. Have the class say the lines as if they were happy or sad, excited or angry, tired or bored.

The students enjoy having their names spotlighted even if the rhyme is nonsensical. To keep track of which names have already been used, place a small mark on the back of the name tag as it is included on the rhyme sheet.

Simple *sol-mi* or *sol-mi-la* pitches can be added to the rhymes to create a song, and published songs that feature children's names are also available. Some can be adapted for use as a question-and-answer song between the teacher and the class. "Who wore brown shoes, brown shoes, brown shoes...?" The child with brown shoes stands up. The class sings "Thad wore brown shoes..." This helps children learn colors, too, along with plaids and stripes.

The class can create its compositions based on the students' names. Four students can choose a rhythm instrument and create a composition with a specific form: AABBCCDD (each child plays the rhythm of his or her name twice), ABCDCBA (rondo form), or ABACDC (two three-part forms). Pitched bar instruments can be used or sound can also be used to create the composition. When the class is familiar with the possibilities, divide them into small groups of four or five, and let each group create its own composition using any sound source.

Many of these activities can be developed into games. Tape a name tag on the back of each child and have him or her try to guess it by asking class members to clap its rhythm. This could be done with one person at a time in front of the class or by the whole group asking one another. The first child to guess the name on his or her back is the winner.

Each of these activities allows children to participate in a worthwhile musical experience while helping teachers learn their students' names. Creative music teachers will be able to find many appropriate music activities that demonstrate their understanding of the importance of what's in a name.

Organization Beyond the Textbooks

by Carolyn Alexander

Most music educators know that successful teaching means more than simply following textbooks from cover to cover. The lessons they plan, the materials they use, and the goals they set can be influenced by anything from current events, to the weather, to the newest show on television. Here are some ideas that may help the beginning music educator organize all the extra duties that become a part of the job.

Gather some information and background on your students. Do students come from rural or metropolitan areas? Do students and their families attend concerts, ballet performances, plays, and museums on their own? Do any of your students study musical instruments, dance, or drama outside of school? Are any parents of your students involved in developing and furthering the arts in your community? Do the parents of your students consider the arts an integral part of general education or a frill?

The answers to these and similar questions may help you understand where your students are in their music education and where they might need to go.

Carolyn Alexander is a music specialist at The Lovett School in Atlanta, Georgia. This article originally appeared in the January 1981 Music Educators Journal.

Make Lists, Establish Rules

Organize your students within each class by keeping lists. If you are using textbooks or other materials that are distributed each time the class meets, keep a list of the class members and let each person take a turn at being in charge of this task. I have also found that a second list is helpful to make sure everyone eventually has a turn to play the special, one-of-a-kind instruments that we have in the classroom. Otherwise, certain students may try to monopolize the bass xylophone, Vibraslap, and temple blocks.

Once rules for behavior and participation have been established for the year, create a visible system of awards so that all classes know where they stand. One strategy that has worked very well with my own students is a chart that lists the names of each class with blocks beside the names that represent each week of the semester. When the students display good behavior and active participation during the week, a block is colored beside the name of the class. At the end of the semester, the class having the most colored blocks receives a prize.

Another idea that can help the music educator who is responsible for a large number of students is to keep a card file on students who seem to have trouble hearing, seeing, behaving, or following instructions in class. When these problems persist over a period of time, this written daily record makes it easier for the teacher to explain low grades, or it may even lead to the discovery that a student has a problem that needs professional help.

Stay Informed, Collect Materials

Be aware of musical happenings around the world. Magazines such as *Time* and *Newsweek* often publish articles about people who are involved in music now as well as about musicians from the past. Bring these articles into your classroom when they are appropriate. Look ahead in television publications and point out to your students special concerts, plays, operas, or other shows they can view at home. You need not restrict their television viewing to music shows. Mime, ballet, and special shows on individual performers or art forms can all contribute to your students' appreciation and understanding of the arts in general.

Turn on your radio, and listen to the music your students hear every day. Teaching with some works, especially themes from current movies that offer interesting studies in rhythm, mood, and orchestration, can add an extra dimension to your music teaching.

Build a file of supplementary teaching materials. Even the best music textbooks may not contain all the information you want to give your students, so build your own library of magazine articles, old textbooks, reference copies of music, and special song collections. If you don't own enough extra materials to begin your library, look around. Visit regional, state, and local conferences for music educators. Representatives of music textbook publishers will often give free materials relating to their books, or even copies of the books themselves, to interested teachers. Check closets or book rooms in your school for old music books that may contain songs no longer included in newer editions. Look through periodicals for educators, and write for free advertised materials. Check through your own piano, instrumental, or vocal literature for selections that can be used in the classroom to study composers or to explore composition ideas.

When these materials have been collected, don't stash them in a closet. Make separate files for units you may study, now or in the future, and fill the files with articles, reference copies, pictures, and index cards giving page numbers of specific books where more information on the subject can be found. After successful units have been taught, add to the files any worksheets or tests that you may want to use again.

Record Accomplishments, Prepare for the Future

Create a visible and audible record of your accomplishments. Make a file or scrapbook containing leaflets from holiday and spring programs. Include photographs of people involved, along with their names and how they contributed to the program. If possible, make tape recordings of performances, and keep them so you can best hear and evaluate the progress that has been made over a period of time. This idea also applies to special projects done in general music classes that may benefit others.

Prepare for the future. When you have established the priorities within your school's music department make an effort to lead the youngest students in those directions. If your school produces a music extravaganza each spring, for instance, give students experiences with moving, singing, playing instruments, and acting at every level. Don't expect vocal soloists to appear suddenly in junior high school if students in elementary school were never given an opportunity to solo. If you count jazz ensembles among the special activities in your school, let students learn improvisation and syncopation long before they arrive with saxophone in hand.

Advertise what you and your students do. How many times have you heard a play-by-play description of the previous evening's football game during your school's morning announcements? Every person who scored a point or assisted in scoring a point for the team is mentioned. Give the same special attention to the musically talented students in your school. When a special performance group gives a concert in or out of school, let everyone know about it. When soloists are needed in a program, hold auditions and announce the winners as proudly as the football coach acknowledges the player who scored the winning touchdown. When your school holds assemblies, plan occasionally for your music groups to be a part of the program. Varied performance opportunities will keep them working diligently throughout the year.

Be prepared for anything. No matter how organized you may be, things go wrong. Always have a backup lesson just in case the equipment you need disappears, the projector bulb goes out, the film you ordered does not arrive on time, or the electricity goes off. Make a collection of games and activities that can be used as time fillers or as complete lessons.

In Case You're Not There...

To be most fully prepared, every teacher should face the fact that he or she may become ill and a substitute will be required to teach the classes. Many substitutes feel uncomfortable in a music class because they don't know the subject matter well enough to teach it. Before you face this prob-

lem, prepare an emergency folder that anyone could use to teach your classes. Include copies of games, such as crossword puzzles, hidden words, or pictures created with music symbols. These will allow the substitute to help review or learn important music terms and signs. For older students, prepare lists of questions and answers that a substitute can use for competitive games in the classroom. If you are ambitious, make cassette recordings with instructions and complete lesson plans on them. Any substitute you call will be more likely to come back again if you make the job as easy as possible.

Each of these ideas takes some extra preparation time, but the benefits can help make your job easier in the long run and can provide your students with the best opportunities to learn.

Section

To Succeed: Active Learning

Elementary music instruction is organized around the content of music—the concepts of melody, rhythm, harmony, and so on. A developmental approach to teaching these musical concepts suggests the need to include extensive concrete experiences during the primary years. This active and experiential involvement then provides a foundation for the eventual teaching of abstractions. Some curriculum authorities believe that, at every level, each lesson should focus on several musical concepts, since music itself comprises many concepts. Other writers espouse an approach whereby one musical concept is the focus of an entire lesson. There is no disagreement, however, regarding the need for the active involvement of children in music making while they develop an overall conceptual framework.

The activities of singing, listening, moving, creating, playing, and music reading are often described as means by which music is taught to children. Understanding how to incorporate these varied ways of musical expression into lessons is an important part of elementary music teacher preparation. Good teaching, however, is never focused solely on activities. Instruction must always be structured so that the activities result in music learning.

READING

In 1838, public school music gained initial support from the Boston School Committee after Lowell Mason had taught without pay in Hawes School for eight months. Through a public demonstration, Mason proved to the committee that the children were capable of learning to read music. In the years since 1838, there has been a great deal of debate within the profession over the importance of notational literacy.

In the first of the articles in this subsection, contrasting viewpoints regarding this important topic are clearly delineated. The next two articles contain descriptions of how practicing elementary classroom teachers have taught children to read music notation through the use of ordinary classroom instruments. These authors describe the individualized and small-group instruction that enabled their students to become music readers.

The Music-Reading Dilemma

by Charles A. Elliott

Music educators have long recognized that only a small number of public school students participate in performance-oriented music classes such as band, orchestra, and choir. Even a smaller percentage continue active participation in music after high school graduation.

This fact has created a philosophical issue in the profession that has been argued for years but has yet to be resolved. What should be the content of the public school music class? Should we teach for enjoyment and appreciation through "the musical experience"? Or should the music class resemble an academic course with an emphasis on the technical aspects of music?

Nowhere is this issue more clearly delineated than in music reading. The importance of teaching music-reading skills to children has been debated almost since the inception of public school music. Historically, however, the role of music reading in public school music education has fluctuated between total commitment and almost total neglect.

During the latter part of the nineteenth century, the teaching of music reading was considered to be the primary purpose of public school music.

Shortly after the turn of the century, the "song method" began to win favor with many teachers. This method called for less emphasis on drill and exercises, which have characterized many music-reading methods, and a greater emphasis on singing. "Whether children were able to read music or not, the general spirit of the period gave song singing the first importance, all other values were reduced to secondary positions."[1]

In 1946, the Music Educators National Conference adopted the following resolution at its meeting in Cleveland:

> Despite the growing tendency to give less time and attention to acquiring skill in reading music, we reaffirm our belief in the importance of an ability to perform music easily and accurately from the printed page.

Still, the issue is far from resolved. Many teachers today are adamant in their belief that music-reading skill should be the primary goal of public school music, and others contend that it should be given only minor consideration, if that.

Charles A. Elliott is a professor of music education at the University of South Carolina in Columbia. This article originally appeared in the February 1982 Music Educators Journal.

No!

Those who are opposed to the teaching of skills such as music reading in the public school usually base their arguments on one or more of the following points:

• Only a small percentage of the students attending public schools will ever have use for music-reading skills after graduation. Russ Widoe, in a letter published in the January 1979 *Music Educators Journal*, wrote that "less than 1 percent of American youngsters will ever find any use for notation skill after graduation, [and] that at least 80 percent of the kids will not progress into high school performing groups." On the same topic, Jacob Kwalwasser argued:

> The music reading objective was more defensible when it was introduced almost 150 years ago.... Before the days of the phonograph and the player-piano, to hear music one was obliged either to make it or be within a hearing range of music being made by others. [2]

Considering the technological advances made in recent years in sound recordings and reproduction, it could be argued that Kwalwasser's thesis is even more true today then when this statement was made in 1955.

• To insist on teaching a skill such as music reading to children who can see no use for it usually results in their developing an aversion to music class. Some music classes are actually teaching children to dislike public school music.

• When music reading becomes the principal objective in public school music, it frequently becomes an end in itself. In many instances, this results in classes consisting mostly of drill, with little music making taking place.

• The music-reading objective has never been successful. Even when it received a great deal of emphasis, few children were actually learning to read music fluently. The argument that this situation currently exists gains some support from the *National Assessment of Educational Progress* (Report 03-MU-01, printed by the United States Government Printing Office), which revealed that only a small percentage of the general population could sight-read even a simple melody.

• Because teaching music reading is time-consuming, it should be a low-priority objective.

Yes!

Those who support the teaching of music-reading skills in the public school usually argue that one of the objectives of our music programs should be to produce musically independent students—students who have the skills to continue with music after high school graduation. Thomas B. Gregory writes that a "prime educational goal of any discipline is the development of an independent learner. In music, an obvious prerequisite to independence is the ability to sightread." [3]

In pressing this argument further, we can usually draw a parallel between the necessity for music-reading ability and that of general reading ability:

> [Because] the person who cannot read is deprived of coming to grips with any form of literature for himself, so is the person who cannot read music deprived of active participation in any music that he has not memorized by listening to others. [4]

In addition, there are those who question whether a real understanding of music can be taught without a grasp of certain fundamental skills such as notation and reading. In the May–June 1957 *Music Journal*, Vincent Jones wrote that, while it "is true that a partial appreciation of music can be achieved without the ability to read ... a real understanding is impossible if printed symbols have no meaning." James L. Mursell argued that the teaching of music reading could be justified on the basis that it is a "tool skill" that can lead to a deeper understanding and appreciation of music.

Mursell also presented a compelling argument on the basis of content matter:

> The abandonment of music reading, or even a serious reduction of emphasis on it, would tend to take away the solid content of music education and would tend to make elementary music nothing but mere play. [5]

In the September 1980 issue of *Principal,* Martin Engel argues that many public schools' arts programs are in deep trouble because of a recent trend to deemphasize their solid content. He writes:

> The fact is that if the arts education community *cannot* show that students are learning what teachers are teaching, then they will have trouble justifying their budgets to the school decision makers, and rightly so. Is there an equivalent dramatic-skills score decline? A drawing-from-life score decline? A music-sight-reading score decline? Do we know? Do we care?

Engel argues further that the arts education community should concentrate on the "teachable" aspects of the arts, which include sight-reading. To ignore this will result in a continued trend to trivialize the arts in the public schools, will make it increasingly difficult to justify their existence, and will result in a general arts deemphasis.

Many argue that music reading is a skill that few will use after graduation, but it can also be argued that so few use it because so few *can* use it. In *Music in Education—A Point of View,* Arnold Bentley writes that nineteenth-century English Board Schools were sometimes awarded grants according to how well children could sing and read music:

> Whether all this was a "good thing," I am not sure. Certain it is, however, that under this system choral societies flourished in cities, towns and smaller communities. [6]

Decisions, Decisions

Both sides, of course, raise difficult questions that must be addressed:

- Has music reading become an obsolete skill for the general population?
- Do so few people use music-reading skills outside of the public school setting because they choose not to or because they cannot?
- Would choral societies and other musical activities flourish if music-reading skills became common in the general population?
- Should public school music consist of allowing students to sing about everyday life, with-

out notation and without interference from music teachers in directing them to "good music"? Could such a music program be justified in the public schools?

- Is Engel correct in arguing that the arts in the public schools have become trivialized and are in danger because of a trend toward simplifying programs?
- Historically, have we been as unsuccessful at teaching music-reading skills as the evidence implies? If so, do we know why?
- Do we know if music-reading skills can be taught in groups to the general school population? If so, do we know how?
- Do we understand the process by which a person learns to sight-read?

To respond to the issue of music reading requires the answer to some fundamental questions about the purpose of public school music. If, as a profession, we cannot state precisely what we are about in the public schools, and provide no hard evidence to show that we can accomplish what we say, then our existence in the public schools will be justifiably threatened.

Notes

1. Theodore A. Tellstrom, *Music in American Education—Past and Present* (New York: Holt, Rinehart and Winston, Inc., 1977), pp. 140–41.

2. Jacob Kwalwasser, *Exploring the Music Mind* (New York: Coleman-Ross Company, Inc., 1955), p. 149.

3. Thomas B. Gregory, "The Effect of Rhythmic Notation Variables on Sight-Reading Errors," *Journal of Research in Music Education,* vol. 20, no. 4, p. 462.

4. Arnold Bentley, *Music in Education—A Point of View* (Windsor, England: NFER Publishing Co., Ltd, 1975), p. 47.

5. James L. Mursell, *Music Education Principles and Problems* (New York: Silver Burdett and Co., 1956), pp. 135, 138.

6. Bentley, p. 49.

The Old Story:
Frustrated Students
The New Ending:
Independent Musicians

by Lois N. Harrison

r. Brown, our principal, is an excellent musician. He plays saxophone for club dates, plays a good jazz piano, and used to teach music. He enjoys hearing children perform, but the first day he entered the music room to find our individualized music reading program in full swing, his face turned gray. After his ears had adjusted to the cacophony, he looked around to find students involved in a vast variety of activities. Jody and Neal had music pinned to a bulletin board and were playing a recorder-Autoharp duet. Three children were working at the piano; five melody-bell players had instruments and music positioned along the windowsill; two theorists were helping each other with notes and note names; several singers were combining forces

with an accompanist playing an Autoharp; recorder players were scattered about the room, some working alone, others playing with partners on the ukulele; and several students were waiting their turns to present finished products to the teacher.

Learning at All Levels

The sixth and seventh graders in this program had started their activities months earlier, near the beginning of the school year. The students had been encouraged to purchase plastic recorders so the entire class could begin learning notes. The few students who did not buy recorders were encouraged to sing the note names while the rest of the class played them. The school provided some equipment for the program, including four Autoharps, eight ukuleles, ten melody bells, and two pianos. Most of these were instruments that had been used in previous years, and only the ukuleles were purchased especially for this project. If other equipment had been available, the program might have taken a different direction.

First, the students learned the music by ear, using such songs as "Mary Had a Little Lamb" and "Hot Cross Buns." As soon as a song was mas-

Lois N. Harrison is a professor and chairs the music education department at The Conservatory of Music of the University of the Pacific, Stockton, California. At the time this article was published, she was teaching music at the Deerfield Middle School in Mountainside, New Jersey. This article originally appeared in the May 1976 Music Educators Journal.

tered, the students wrote it down. The teacher gave only as much direction as was absolutely necessary. Most of the early songs were learned in several keys: G, F, A, D, C. Faster classes were able to learn all the keys and write them down. It became evident even in the early stage of the reading program, however, that there were individual differences and therefore individual problems.

The recorder players exhibited a wide range of capability. Some children practiced at home and showed rapid progress in finger dexterity and tone production. Others coupled a lack of practice with coordination difficulties that caused them to move very slowly. Within a few weeks, each class had become stratified internally according to individual rates of progress. Here was the old story: As the class moved along together, those who practiced conscientiously became frustrated because others were not able to move as fast as they could. The slow or poorly prepared students started to fall still farther behind. The progress of the class was just right for very few of the children. The class was working and the sound was quite nice, but much more had to be done for *all* the children.

Colored Sheets for Individual Pacing

During the next phase of the program, the students began to move at individual speeds. Each was given "the orange sheet" (called that only to distinguish it from the other sheets that followed). The orange sheet had on it six melodies or parts of melodies that the children were asked to practice until they were able to play or sing them for the teacher. If they sang them, they were to sing note names. Although all the melodies were familiar ones, no names or words were given on the sheet.

Once again, those who practiced and the conscientious students were quickly ready to play their melodies, but this time they didn't have to wait for the other students. They played each piece that was ready for the teacher, and then either practiced those parts in which they had made mistakes or went on to prepare the next melody. The teacher was able to circulate, giving help to students who needed it. Sometimes fast students were asked to help slower ones.

Some students still had no recorders and were such uncertain singers that, although they had learned the names of pitches, they were unable to reproduce the correct tones. These students responded eagerly to the melody bells. They were encouraged to try playing their pieces on these instruments, which had the names of the notes printed on the metal bars.

As soon as the students finished the orange sheets, they were given green sheets. Where the first materials had been only melodies, the new ones had melodies with chords. The students were asked to work in teams now, with one musician playing or singing the melody and the other accompanying with the Autoharp. These melodies were easier than the first ones and were accompanied by only two chords, G and D7. If students wanted to play these pieces by themselves, they could use the piano.

The next sheet to be added was the yellow sheet. By this time, the students who had finished the first sheets were demonstrating melodic performance ability whether they were playing or singing. They could also read music performed by someone else well enough to change chords at the proper time. Although many students still had not finished the orange and green sheets, those who had were ready for a new stage in their harmonic development. The yellow sheet started them on the ukulele. It acquainted them with the structure of the instrument, the strings, and the playing position.

The blue sheet taught the G and D7 chords on the ukulele and directed the students back to the green sheet. They could either sing these tunes and accompany themselves, or continue working with a partner.

The pink sheet added the D and A7 chords and provided new melodic material. The white sheet continued with more new melodic material using the chords that had already been learned and added the C chord. The last item on this sheet asked students to write their own chords under a given melody.

By the time the fast learners had finished the white sheet, some students had still not finished the orange sheet. Their problems were not only with the music. These were the students who also had difficulty remembering to bring their recorders to class, and they kept losing their sheets. At first, the teacher gave new sheets; later she asked the students to borrow a sheet and hand-copy a new one. An advantage of this program was that no matter how many setbacks of this nature occurred and no matter how often students were absent, they could reenter the program just where they had left off.

When the students came to the teacher to check off their work, they were given help as it was needed. Each child had his or her own needs. No one had to suffer through corrections for things that did not need correcting, nor could anyone get away with errors that were hidden by the good work of others. Best of all, work that was rhythmic and accurate could be applauded.

Time Considerations and Other Caveats

A few cautions about a program of this nature should be considered. The students must be well-grounded in the care of the instruments with which they work. They have to be encouraged to have a cooperative and helpful attitude toward each other. There should be a terminal point for the project so the students don't get the feeling that the same activities will be going on forever. The students respond well to time expectations, such as "you should be able to finish this sheet in six weeks."

The children seem able to concentrate on their own music while everyone else's is going on in the room at the same time. The person who has the greatest difficulty concentrating in the midst of the din may be the music teacher!

This program does not replace group activities entirely. The classes still have singing experiences, and they still listen to music, analyze it, and enjoy it. They have music projects, they dance a little, and they prepare for field trips. Also, near the end of the school year, the classes join together to give a concert for themselves.

What is the student left with at the end of this part of the music-reading program? The word "end" should be used only if it means that the time of immediate concentration is over. No one really gets to the end of a program like this, for there is always one more step to take. Remember, all the students did not finish the same amount of work. Most of them, however, did achieve a basic ability to read melodies. Many of them could add harmonies to these melodies, and most of the students mastered elementary music tools that will help them gain more skill in music reading.

Mr. Brown regained his composure quickly when he looked closely at activities that were creating the din in the music room. He soon saw that these students were functioning as independent musicians. Now, he hardly blanches as he comes through the door.

Recorder Ensembles—A New Wind in the Elementary Program

by Martha A. Giles

Recorder class has been a popular part of the elementary curriculum for many years. It is intended to teach children to read music and help them develop rudimentary skills for band instruments, as well as to introduce them to a folk instrument they can continue playing.

However, the most common methods of organizing the recorder class—homogeneous grouping and individualized instruction—have some serious drawbacks. In homogeneous groupings, students often have trouble hearing themselves, and the teacher has limited opportunity to identify and work on the particular problems of each student. Individual instruction usually depends on students practicing at home, which can lead to students forgetting to bring their instruments or music back to class, and, too frequently, forgetting practicing itself.

Because of these methods' failings, teachers may hesitate to begin recorder classes, doubting their benefits. Students may quickly tire of class because they do not readily develop skills for more advanced music. I have often witnessed the frustrations of both teachers and students in this situation and wondered why mixed ensembles were not developed from the very beginning.

The Benefits of Mixed Ensembles

Mixed ensembles, in which the recorder is used with other classroom instruments, can solve several problems in beginning recorder classes. First, intonation is improved because the student can hear his or her own instrument against the other timbres of the ensemble. Second, the teacher can circulate from ensemble to ensemble, checking on fingerings, breath support, and other problems that might arise. Third, students enjoy the ensemble sound and, it is hoped, will do ensemble work outside of class. A variety of literature can be learned in pleasant arrangements, and there is more opportunity for improvisation. Finally, the recorder can be used as it was intended—as an ensemble instrument.

Structuring the ensemble involves the simple task of dividing the class into groups playing five or six varied instruments, using available classroom folk instruments. If study carrels or practice rooms are not accessible, these ensembles can be scattered around a large room. Students can be taught to play softly enough that they do not interfere with other groups. They soon learn to ignore the sounds

Martha A. Giles teaches in the music department at George Mason University in Fairfax, Virginia. This article originally appeared in the December 1982 Music Educators Journal.

Figure 1. "Mary Had a Little Llama."

of other groups in the room as they become involved in their own ensemble.

Each ensemble should consist of one or two recorders, one or two melodic instruments such as melody bells, guitar, or Autoharp, and percussion instruments such as tambourine, wood or sand blocks, or small drums. Students can take turns practicing instruments within the ensemble so that they develop skills in playing all of the instruments.

Easy and interesting arrangements of well-known melodies or original pieces can be written by the teacher. Take, for example, my arrangement of "Mary Had a Little Lamb," titled "Mary Had a Little Llama" (see Figure 1). This piece does not tax the recorder player or the bell player. The percussionists will be challenged, but the rhythmic motives and ostinatos are so well-known that they can master them quickly. As students gained skills in playing and improvising, they could try writing their own arrangements. The greatest problem to this approach is developing an abundance of easy arrangements; however, such arrangements do not take long to write, and five or six arrangements can keep a class busy for some time as they are circulated from group to group.

Improvisation should be an important part of the ensemble experience. For example, ask the percussionists in the ensembles to work out an ostinato as a basis for a piece. Let us say that there are two percussionists, and they develop two complimentary ostinatos, as follows:

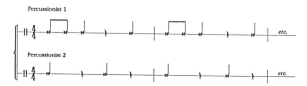

Players of melodic instruments can be given a tonal pentatonic scale such as C, D, F, G, and A on which to improvise. No matter which of these pitches are sounded together, they sound harmonious. Students will feel comfortable playing melodies and countermelodies together. As students learn to play more accidentals, the same type of improvisation can be done with a whole-tone scale. Of course, we should not be afraid to improvise with major and minor scales, or even modes. The half-step intervals and tendency tones in these scales can be assimilated by students if they are given the opportunity to work with them. Students learn so much intuitively, especially when they are given aural experiences; besides, a little dissonance won't hurt them.

The Importance of Ear Training

The key to a successful recorder program is aural training. The child's ability to hear the musical tone, motif, phrase, and so on is essential to development of other skills for playing a recorder. The common method of teaching students in a homogeneous grouping is inadequate because the student cannot hear his or her own tone properly. Try playing your recorder with cotton in your ears—a frustrating experience, but similar to the one homogeneous groupings produce. Better still, sit down in the midst of your recorder class while they are playing, and try to distinguish one sound from another. It is difficult.

Finally, the ensemble approach to the recorder class establishes the kind of environment for which the recorder was intended. Most general music students will not become professional musicians when they grow up. They should be shown not only how the recorder was used historically, but how it can be used in the future. I hope that your students will enjoy your recorder class so much that they will continue playing in their own recorder ensembles long after they leave your classroom.

SINGING

Music instruction in American public schools was initially and primarily based on a singing approach. The articles in this subsection focus on a variety of approaches that can help children become skillful, musical, and enthusiastic singers. These authors believe that it is a music teacher's responsibility to provide instructional opportunities whereby all children can become successful singers. This type of instruction includes providing a conducive environment for children to experiment with and through which they can discover their own singing voices. General music teachers also need to give students opportunities to sing together in large groups. Although Mary Goetze's article may seem to pertain only to performance groups, her belief that elementary choirs should be for all children makes her comments about literature selection and presentation, modeling, and chorister selection particularly pertinent.

A Responsibility to Young Voices

by Peggy D. Bennett

I f I were to ask you "Under what conditions does your singing voice sound its *best?*" what would you answer?

"In the shower."
"When I'm rested."
"In a certain key."
"When I'm relaxed."
"When I'm confident about what I'm singing."
"When I sing with a 'good' singer."
"When no one is listening."
All of the above?

Or what if I asked the opposite question—"When does your singing sound its *worst?*" When you are nervous, uncomfortable, threatened, afraid, tired, ill, embarrassed, bored, or have allergies? Being aware of the conditions that work for or against a natural, desirable vocal tone is the first step in creating a classroom environment conducive to voice education.

Responsibility to Voices

I am an instrumentalist. Although I have taught children and adults using a vocal approach to studying music for fifteen years, only recently have

Peggy D. Bennett is an associate professor and head of music at the University of Texas at Arlington. This article was originally published in the September 1986 Music Educators Journal.

I realized how little attention I have paid to voices in my classrooms. Where once I saw my own voice and the students' voices simply as necessary instruments for producing songs and communicating instructions and ideas, I now realize that I have a very critical responsibility with my students: to help them find and maintain a comfortable, healthy speaking and singing voice. Awareness of this responsibility has led me to reconsider ways voices are used in music classes.

> If asked, can you stand up and ... prove that your major concern as a professional entrusted with young voices ... has always been and will always be the well-being of the instruments you work with?
>
> Do you think you presently would be judged "guilty" or "not guilty" if standing accused of injuring—temporarily or permanently—one of the voices you accepted to use in one of your projects? [1]

The issues of choral singing, diction, technical voice information, and vocal abuse are not addressed here. Rather, ideas, teaching strategies, and activities will be offered that can contribute to vocal awareness, production, and maintenance for the nonselect general music student.

A Conducive Environment

Student's voices should be treated as carefully as their minds and bodies are treated. Psychological stress seems to have an effect on a person's voice. "A vocal athlete's reaction to environmental stress can affect her/his singing ability. A common term for stress reaction is 'fight or flight response.'"[2] The positive, accepting attitude the teacher models toward students and voices is most effective if the selected songs and activities are complementary to that attitude.

Positive attitudes to model include a curiosity about and a respect for voices that express interest in what voices can do, not how "good" they sound; a stance that discourages laughing or teasing when voices are studied; and an acceptance of each voice as it is, recognizing that "all voices are good and are in different stages of learning, growing, and improving."[3]

Complementary songs are those that have variety in tonal and rhythmic patterns; are simple in their tonal progressions; closely resemble natural speech in their tonal and rhythmic setting of words; are appealing and interesting for children to sing; and have a vitality not diminished by extended repetition.

Complementary activities motivate students to participate; provide opportunities for students to offer ideas and see their ideas implemented; give students responsibility in the ongoing flow and "working" of the group and the activity; focus students on the song or activity for maximum learning; and offer movement to encourage, not impede, healthy vocal production and flow of the song.

Such compliments as, "That sounds good," or "What a pretty voice you have," are seldom appropriate for voice education. Instead, more appropriate feedback encourages and supports, rather than compliments:

> "I can hear that your voice sounds more relaxed today."
>
> "It sounds as if your voice is not accustomed to that range."
>
> "Your voice sounded like you were really supporting it with energy this time."

Again, the curiosity for what a voice can do and appreciation of a student's efforts in exploring his or her voice underlie the teacher attitude being modeled for the class. Consistency with this attitude can offer students the emotional safety necessary to explore the potential of their voices in the presence of their classmates.

Phases of Voice Education

There are six phases of vocal awareness. Although these phases are somewhat sequential, progress through them may move very quickly. In voice education, each student:

1. Experiments with the quality and range possibilities of his or her voice;

2. Describes how his or her voice feels as he or she experiments, where he or she feels the voice on his or her body as he or she experiments, and how his or her and others' voices sound as they experiment;

3. Matches quality and range of the teacher and other students in singing or speaking activities;

4. Decides which labels best fit a given vocal production of his or her and another's voice (for instance, "high," "medium," or "low"; "loud," "medium," or "quiet");

5. Produces a particular sound according to a given label ("high," "soft," "smooth," and so on).

6. Produces a specific pitch to match one given by another voice or instrument.

Unfortunately, the sequence for working with children's voices frequently begins at step 6: "Okay, class, sing this note," or, "Tommy, you're not matching my pitch; sing higher." Typically, pitch matching has been seen as an essential prerequisite skill to music instruction. So valued has this ability been to many general music teachers that students' musical abilities have often been summarized in terms of whether they match pitch.

The ability to sing one pitch to match precisely another produced by voice or instrument may be *more* surprising to find than the inability to do so. There are many mechanical reasons for the inability to match pitches, and the ear seldom is the culprit. Although matching pitch is certainly one of the goals of voice education, it is not the first step—nor is it the ultimate step of vocal health, production, and awareness.

Another common strategy in teaching singing is to emphasize the concepts of "high" and "low" in relation to pitch level. Perhaps it is time to reevaluate this strategy, as the term "high" refers to the *visual* representation of notes on the staff—not a workable concept for many young children. Physically, "higher" notes on the piano are to the right of "lower" notes; on the violin, they are closer to the player's body; on the guitar, they are *beneath* the "lower" notes. Acoustically, "higher" actually means "faster." Physiologically, "higher" does not correctly describe what happens in the vocal mechanism as higher pitches are produced. Furthermore, the image of reading and the postural tension that can result from acting out high and low notes can impede proper functioning of the vocal mechanism to produce these sounds.

Instead of eliminating such terms as "high" or "low" from teaching strategies used with young children, teachers should work toward this fifth phase of development through the students' perceptions (see step 4). Perhaps teachers have forced a framework of extremes of opposites ("high" versus "low") onto a simple activity like singing that does not need such a confining structure.

First, Experimentation

In this initial phase of voice exploration, the speaking voice may be a more comfortable starting point than the singing voice. In addition, some research indicates that the speaking voice may be a more *logical* beginning for voice education than the singing voice. Betty Atterbury summarized these conclusions in an article in *MEJ*:

> [A. Oren] Gould emphasized in his conclusion that a most important initial step in teaching singing was to enable children to differentiate register changes in their speaking voices. This finding was also emphasized by two later authors, Emlyn Roberts and Ann D. M. Davies in their research with ninety nonsingers.

They wrote that the breakthrough with individual nonsingers seemed to occur when the children realized they could control the pitch fluctuation in their own voices.[4]

One exercise for exploring the speaking voice in quality and register involves the recitation of a familiar song or poem—for instance, "Mary Had a Little Lamb." Have the students speak the poem, not necessarily trying to stay together. After the class has simply recited the poem a few times, suggest imagery to guide them to different types of vocal production through interpretation:

> "This time as you say the poem, pretend you are a very important actor, alone on the stage, very confident, enjoying your time in the spotlight."
>
> "Now pretend you are a very shy student approaching a stern principal."
>
> "Pretend you are a storyteller trying to make the story come alive for this audience."

Have all students practice speaking as a group with each new image; offering several repetitions gives students ample opportunity to explore their interpretations. In addition, using a familiar song or poem gives a definite framework for the voice exploration. Unlike some activities where environmental sounds are explored, the familiar text gives a predictable, predetermined stopping point.

When students are ready, have them give their own interpretation for the group. This may be a difficult or embarrassing step for some students. Encouraging, supportive interest from the teacher can create the necessary components of social comfort and studious curiosity for the student "soloists."

> "Todd, I heard an interesting voice from you that time. Would you let us all listen?"
>
> "I'd like to hear several ideas, so when I gesture to you, give us your interpretation. We won't respond or comment until we have heard from four or five of you."

And, for getting started with this type of activity in an unusually inhibited class:

> "Just so you can get accustomed to speaking alone for the group, we'll close our eyes while we listen. When I tap your shoulder, give us your own interpretation."

Anna Peter Langness, in her writings on the child voice, emphasizes:

> Individuals are invited and encouraged, never threatened nor forced, to speak or sing alone! Assume that if a student is not ready at this moment, he/she may respond later this song, this period, next class, or next week. Always extend the invitation, or find an opportunity when the entire class is not listening. [5]

Step 2: Description

Encourage students to comment on what they heard and how they could describe the voices—how it felt to produce certain voices and how it sounded as they listened. Take time to allow students to explain their comments, demonstrate what they mean, and express varying points of view. As stated earlier, their statements should not express liking or dislike.

> "Dawn, how could you describe what you heard in Sandy's voice that time? [Student responds.] How would you describe it, Sean? [Student responds.] Well, Sandy, you've heard various people describe what they heard in your voice; why don't you tell us how it *felt* for you to speak that way?"

When a student's response is vague, unclear, or seemingly "off the wall," give him or her more opportunity to clarify:

> "Joe, I'm not quite sure what you are saying. Could you tell me a little more about what you mean?"
> "Jennifer, I am curious about what you just

said. Let me listen again so I can make sure I'm understanding you."

> "Todd, can you tell me more about what you're saying? [Pause; no response.] Well, maybe you just need more thinking time to put your thoughts into words. Be sure to let me know when you can tell me more about your idea."

If student verbalizations of their own ideas are uncommon for the classroom, a little time may be needed for them:

- to realize that the teacher is asking for their opinions and perceptions rather than for a "correct" answer;
- to listen to and study responses of other students in addition to those of the teacher;
- to appreciate "playing with voices" as a serious yet enjoyable study in music education;
- to value similar answers given by several students but articulated in various ways.

Once again, the teacher is a valuable model for each of these adjustments.

Matching Quality and Range

Antiphonal response is a strategy that works well for imitating speaking and singing voices. With a song well-known to the group, a leader begins speaking or singing the words. At various points in the text, the leader stops speaking and the group must fill in the missing words. Whenever the leader comes back in with the song, the group must stop speaking or singing. Unlike an echoing activity, antiphonal response recreates the song intact from beginning to end. It is more a game of "fill in the blanks" than one of "do what I do." The aim is to have as smooth and musical a transition as possible between the leader and followers.

After the students have explored and described the various speaking voices produced with imaging on "Mary Had a Little Lamb," name one student to be the leader, and have the rest of the class respond antiphonally. Instruct the students to try to match the vocal quality and range of the leader.

Some laughing or teasing may occur as students hear and use voices in ways new to them. Although laughter may simply reflect embarrassment or delight, it should be minimized. The teacher can recognize the class's sense of humor and at the same time limit the students' laughter:

> "I know it sounds comical to us to use these voices, and rather surprising, too. During voice study, we cannot laugh. If we laugh, it may be too easy for a person to think we're laughing at *them*, and we don't want to do that."

Continual reinforcement of the "no laughing" rule may be necessary in beginning voice study.

> Humor and acknowledgement of some discomfort helps the children relax and respond freely. "This is kinda crazy!" or "What IS this?" may be patterns that express what the children are thinking, and [they allow] that feeling to be acceptable without interfering with the progress of the work. [6]

As a variety of vocal ranges and qualities are experienced among the group, students are again encouraged to describe how the voices felt and sounded. Discussing these two perceptions separately accepts that one student may feel his or her vocal production as normal, and another may hear that same production as a quiet voice. Likewise, a student may *hear* a voice as being loud, yet when he or she matches that voice with his or her own, it may not *feel* loud.

Making use of students' comments on their perceptions heightens vocal awareness. Rather than assign descriptors to students' voices, the teacher allows students to discover the breadth of range and quality in the human voice. One of the principles suggested for learning to use the singing voice satisfactorily is "the child must learn to hear, judge, and control his [or her] own voice." [7] Among the concepts and associated motor skills necessary to young children's singing abilities, is "a concept of the difference between high sounds and low sounds and the motor skill of con-

trolling the pitch levels of the voice in speech and song." [8]

Deciding on Labels

As stated earlier, students may not find the concepts of "high" and "low" in reference to musical pitches and ranges as obvious as we teachers might think. When discussing vocal ranges and qualities, the teacher can eventually introduce the question of:

> "Laura, when you sang [spoke] that, did it *feel* like you used your high voice, low voice, or medium voice? [Student responds.] Pam, did Laura's voice *sound* high, medium, or low to you?"

"High," "low," "medium," "medium high," and "medium low" are frameworks of register decided upon by the students about their own voices. The variety of descriptors also recognizes the difficulty of placing any sound into discrete categories of high and low. In this way, voice education with regard to blending registers and establishing comfortable ranges becomes individualized instruction within the group setting. These personal range descriptors also become frames of reference for the next step in voice education.

Matching Sound to Label

After students have offered their own labels for various qualities of their and other's voices, transition to responding to a request for a specific sound evolves easily.

> "Jonathan, was that your high, medium, or low voice I heard that time? [Response: "Low."] Well, how would it sound if you used your high voice to sing [speak] that? [Response: Student sings in high voice.] Wow! I heard the difference! Now, I wonder what your medium voice would sound like. Can you show me?"

For this type of voice study, short phrases (for example, "the lamb was sure to go" or "who lives in Drury Lane") are often more appropriate than entire songs or poems. Also, when a student seems stuck in a particular range (usually low), quickly insert an echoing activity. The teacher models a quickly paced, energetic speaking voice, accompanied by gestures.

> "Chris, let's try this. See if you can echo me. We're on top of a mountain, and we're thrilled to be there. 'Hello-o-o-o.' [Response.] 'Hello-o-o-o, is anybody there?' [Response.] 'What is your name?' "

During this improvisation, a spontaneity of response to the student's echoes is required of the teacher. Repeating, varying, stretching words and syllables, and accompanying these with gestures and facial expressions can help the student exercise in a range unfamiliar to his or her voice. If exercise becomes too focused on the one student, have the entire class join in. As soon as the student can, have him or her use his or her high voice without a teacher model.

> "Can you tell me what your voice had to do in order to get that high sound?"
>
> "Did your high voice feel any different from your low voice? How?"

Eventually, the use of such questions can aid students in monitoring their vocal production for singing or speaking in class and for practice at home. Betty Atterbury says, "A vital element in successful primary singing instruction is the consistent inclusion of some activities that enable children to differentiate their individual voice registers." [9]

Producing a Given Pitch

This final step in voice education is so common it needs little explanation. Probably most of our class time focuses on this step. Inadequate experience in any of the previous five steps, however, can impede success with "matching pitch."

Some elementary music teachers may work with students through seven years of physical growth and development. Growth and development, so

obvious in external characteristics, also occur within the vocal mechanism. "Matching pitch" may be a skill that varies according to physical growth. As children grow in and out of voice coordination—ear-throat coordination—it is imperative that their voices and voice images be treated with care.

The Living Voice

Voices are produced by a system of living tissue. They need to be as carefully exercised, nourished, warmed up, explored, used, and maintained as the rest of our bodies must be.

> The vocal "instrument" is not an instrument, although we use voices for that purpose. Musical instruments are inanimate objects [that] are used as extensions of human beings. Guitars do not catch colds. Tuba players do not play their tubas to carry on daily conversation.
>
> Voices are human beings. They are made up of living tissues that are part of the whole human being's physical and psychical processes. When misused, they may fall into "disrepair." Replacement voices cannot be purchased at the local music store, and there [are] no such thing[s] as "trade-ins." Vocal "repair" is possible, up to a point, but loaners for temporary use while repair is under way are not [available]. [10]

Voices also represent who we are to ourselves and to those around us. Robbing someone of confidence in—or of the opportunity to become confident in—his or her singing or speaking voice, by intended or implied remarks, diminishes his or her quality of life.

> And so what, you're saying? You don't seek power, fame, or glory? Your aspirations are less lofty? Well, the principles still apply to you. I've never met a person who didn't want to be liked. Who didn't want to be listened to. Who didn't want to be appreciated for his or her individuality. And that individuality—that specialness that is you—is what we're aiming to reveal in your voice.

Therein lies the essence of my message to you: Your voice is your personal trademark. It serves as a calling card, presenting you and your ideas and your personality to a judgmental world, a world that will remember your voice image as vividly as your physical image, and perhaps more vividly. [11]

Reminders for Voice Educators

Music teachers have a unique potential for aiding proper, healthy vocal production and maintenance. Sensitivity toward the child's voice and his or her own voice image can be a first step toward taking this responsibility. A second step requires curiosity to learn more about voices and to analyze what is asked of voices in our classroom.

Here are five suggestions that could serve as reminders in beginning exercises for vocal awareness and education:

1. Substitute the phrase "sing with more energy" for "sing louder."
2. Get a vitality, flow, and freedom in the singing of a song before focusing on the students' individual voices.
3. Incorporate simple movement and gestures to accompany the energy level given to the speaking and singing voice.
4. Avoid overemphasizing the concepts of "high" and "low" as a means for instructing children to shift pitches or registers. Without students' personal awareness of the physical changes that occur, this can be detrimental to proper use of the vocal mechanism.
5. Remember that the experiences inherent in each of the six steps outlined earlier add up to something greater than the mere achievement of the last step, matching pitch.

Ultimately, the student's self is more important than musical skills he or she does or does not possess. It is this self that, if properly cared for, can unleash new potential for vocal facility in speaking and singing.

Notes

1. Axel Theimer, "What if...? Some Thoughts for Us to Whom Young Voices are Entrusted," *The Choral Journal*, January 1982, 31.

2. Leon Thurman, "Putting Horses Before Carts: When Choral Singing Hurts Voices," *The Choral Journal*, April 1983, 23.

3. Anna Peter Langness, "The Child Voice," 16 (Unpublished research paper, available from the author: Music Study Services, PO Box 4665, Englewood, CO 80155, 1983).

4. Betty Atterbury, "Are You Really Teaching Children *How* to Sing?" *Music Educators Journal* 70, no. 8, April 1984, 44.

5. Langness, 17.

6. Langness, 23.

7. Elda Franklin and David Franklin, "The Uncertain Singer," *Update: The Applications of Research in Music Education* 1, no. 3, Spring 1983, 4.

8. Franklin and Franklin, 4.

9. Atterbury, 44.

10. Thurman, 23.

11. Morton Cooper, *Change Your Voice, Change Your Life* (New York: Macmillan, 1984), 51.

Selected Readings

Apfelstadt, Hilary. "Children's Vocal Range: Research Findings and Implications for Music Education." *Update: The Applications of Research in Music Education* 1, no. 2, Fall 1982, 3-7.

Gould, A. Oren. "Developing Specialized Programs for Singing in the Elementary School." *Bulletin of the Council for Research in Music Education*, no. 17, 1969, 9-22.

Are You Really Teaching Children *How* to Sing?

by Betty W. Atterbury

Educators can accept the premise that children who are unsuccessful in arithmetic in the primary grades and who develop negative attitudes toward math, perhaps even "math phobias," will not be interested in taking math courses in secondary school. Considering the importance of singing in most elementary general music classrooms, it is not surprising that a primary child who is an unsuccessful singer and who is never taught *how* to sing will develop a similar negative attitude and a parallel lack of interest in participating in any music courses.

The current budget cuts and possible continued budget restrictions have served as an impetus for justifying music programs. In addition to constantly depressing budget realities, the steadily declining student population has presented music educators with another threat to programs that include small numbers of students. Perhaps instead of more justification, more defenses, and more public relations, an alternative approach is needed. A consideration of the impact that the complete music program has on students that included curriculum

Betty W. Atterbury is an associate professor of music education at the University of Southern Maine in Gorham. This article originally appeared in the April 1984 Music Educators Journal.

and instructional changes might better increase the numbers of future students who elect to participate in music programs.

Music educators who are separated by building and age-level demarcations become so involved in preparing and presenting seasonal concerts and trying to survive budget cuts that they do not direct enough thought to ensuring long-range survival, improvement, and expansion of music programs. Consideration of a curriculum continuum from kindergarten through grade 12 would include a restructuring of the factors that cause negative student attitudes and large program dropout rates. One excellent beginning step would be to teach all young children *how* to sing.

Absolved of Responsibility

The omission of planned programs in singing may have evolved because of two contrasting views of children's vocal development. One of the traditional approaches to teaching children includes a belief that the ability to sing is innate. It has been found that children in kindergarten who sing well usually come from musical environments. The reason the remainder of the kindergarten class cannot sing on pitch, however, is not that they are untalented. They simply have not ever been taught *how* to sing!

A second rationale for not teaching singing was exemplified in the article "Monotonism" by Elda

Franklin (March 1981 *MEJ*, pp. 56-59), in which the author suggested that the inability to sing (or "monotonism") may be a neurological disorder of the right hemisphere of the brain. Both rationales—innate talent and neurological dysfunction—lead to the same conclusion: the reasons for poor singing ability are found within the child. These beliefs serve to absolve the music teacher of any responsibility for instruction in the basic musical activity used in the primary grades—singing.

Many authorities in music education believe, however, that every child can be taught to sing. Edwin Gordon wrote that "anyone can learn to sing, just as anyone can learn to talk."[1] Many skilled music specialists concur and insist that by the end of second grade there should be no out-of-tune singers. These statements imply that singing is a teachable skill, and researchers who have worked with poor singers agree. Several authors have concluded that the important time for teaching children how to sing is while children are young. Unfortunately, textbooks currently available for use in the primary grades do not include a structured approach to teaching young children how to sing.[2] Therefore, general music teachers need to be aware of the necessary components involved in teaching singing to young children and incorporate them in their primary lesson planning.

Aware of Their Own Voices

Research that has included nonsinging subjects has some important conclusions and implications for singing instruction. One long-term project in young children's singing ability was concluded by A. Oren Gould in 1969.[3] The three-year project focused on how children learn to sing and included surveys of successful teachers of singing plus two yearlong research projects with unsuccessful young singers. Gould emphasized in his conclusion that a most important initial step in teaching singing was to enable children to differentiate register changes in their speaking voices. This finding was also emphasized by two later authors, Emlyn Roberts and Ann D. M. Davies, in their research with ninety nonsingers.[4] They wrote that the breakthrough with individual nonsingers seemed

to occur when the children realized they could control the pitch fluctuations in their own voices.

How can the findings of these researchers best be incorporated into lesson planning for primary children? Activities that emphasize vocal and register differences should be included in every lesson. Common suggestions found in most methods' texts include having children whisper, speak, and sing using the same verbal material: rhymes, chants, or improvised sentences. Imitation of environmental sounds is another excellent device that enables young children to experience changes in their own vocal registers. Children enjoy pretending to be the wind or a fire engine and moving their arms or entire bodies up and down with the sound.

Another activity is rhythmically speaking known nursery rhymes and then singing them on one pitch. When all the children can successfully sing on one tone, the same activity can be extended to include a descending minor third and other intervals.

A vital element in successful primary singing instruction is the consistent inclusion of some activities that enable children to differentiate their individual voice registers. Including a fire engine imitation in every week's lesson, however, will not enable any child to become a successful singer. The activity needs to be accompanied by the child's active awareness of the physical changes that occur when they speak and when they sing. Music teachers need to have young children touch their own throats when they are making register changes with their voices. This type of active involvement increases the rate of successful singing participation. Teachers who demonstrate and briefly explain how and why the voice changes enable children to focus on vocal experimentation and eventually attain success in this necessary aspect of learning how to sing.

Develop Tonal Memory

A second finding from music education research indicates that learning to sing requires an increase in the ability to recognize and remember melody. One research report that described the training of eleven-year-old nonsingers included a conclusion that the development of the individual subject's musical memory paralleled his or her ability to sing on pitch.[5] Methods textbooks that discuss teaching young children how to sing have not focused on this important singing development factor.

Activities that increase children's melodic memory need to be consistently incorporated into primary music lesson planning. One effective teaching method that enables young children to develop a tonal memory is to introduce known songs in every lesson with only a melody instrument, such as a recorder. Other activities include singing echoes and playing echoes on xylophones, both of which assist children in remembering tonal patterns. With practice, these echoes can be lengthened, enabling children to extend their tonal memories.

Some traditional formats for teaching primary music may not be compatible with the development of melodic awareness and memory. Helmut Moog found that children through age five are not auditorily aware of harmony.[6] This finding implies that one may best plan most primary singing instruction without accompaniment. Although the recordings that accompany current texts contain attractive and varied arrangements for adult listeners, the same sounds may not contribute to the development of melodic awareness and subsequent singing ability for young children. It has been suggested that teachers not use a piano when teaching primary grades, as the amount of sound overwhelms the voices of young singers. Another reason to avoid the piano is that primary children cannot easily distinguish the foreground (melody) from the background (harmony). Without the development of an internal awareness and recognition of melody and its components—register, direction, and contour—tonal memory will not develop adequately.

Choose Limited Range

The most important influence a music teacher can have on young children's voice development is in the selection of song material with an appropriate range and tessitura. Gordon suggested that songs with extreme ranges and tessituras contribute to the development of nonsingers. Many teach-

ers of primary classes become immune to the "droning" sounds produced by children who do not sing in the range of printed music. This phenomenon does not usually disappear as children become older, but it could be partially eliminated by choosing songs that encompass a comfortable range.

What is the best range for young children? A review of the research literature from 1895 to 1977 conducted by Graham F. Welch revealed that most authors agree on a primary-age range of a fifth or sixth.[7] Welch also reported research agreement that the vocal center of this range is middle C, C-sharp, or D. These findings have not been incorporated into the overall selection of songs in texts for young children. Table 1 shows the results of an informal survey of kindergarten and first-grade music books to determine the percentages of songs with limited ranges (a third to a sixth) and wider ranges (a seventh to a ninth or tenth). Although all textbooks contain some songs with a limited range, they contain many more songs that are inappropriate for young children's singing voices. Obviously, music teachers need to be extremely selective in their use of these textbooks when planning singing experiences for young children.

The presence of a small vocal range in young children has two implications for planning and teaching in the primary grades. First, teachers should only choose songs for young children that the children can sing successfully. These songs should have a range of no more than a fifth or sixth. Second, the songs selected should center around middle C. This means that songs including C or D on the treble clef should be transposed or ignored!

It seems that the rationale for printing so many songs for young children in inappropriate singing keys is a belief that general music teachers lack an extensive piano technique. Songs can be found in current textbooks that have small ranges but are printed and recorded to accommodate piano accompaniments in the keys of F or G. The use of such arrangements is not recommended because they will not provide successful experiences for children learning how to sing. If the research finding regarding children's inability to discriminate melody and harmony is accurate, the music teacher

Table 1
Percentages of Songs with Limited and Wide Ranges from Selected Music Books

Title	Limited range	Wide range
The Music Book		
(Holt, Rinehart and Winston, 1981)		
Kindergarten	32	68
Grade 1	47	53
Silver Burdett Music		
(Silver Burdett, 1981)		
Kindergarten	36	64
Grade 1	35	65
The Spectrum of Music		
(Macmillan, 1980)		
Kindergarten	32	68
Grade 1	34	66

who is concerned with teaching every child how to sing will not be influenced by the printed piano accompaniment, but will select songs with appropriately small ranges and low tessituras.

To Teach Each Child

Research conducted with nonsingers contains repeated conclusions that the ideal age to teach children how to sing is in the primary grades. Because current textbooks do not include sequenced material that can be used to develop children's singing ability, general music teachers should incorporate the types of activities described into their short- and long-term planning. In addition, careful selection of songs used in primary classes is highly recommended. A short list of songs with appropriate ranges for young children is found in *Music in the Elementary School* (Robert Evans Nye and Vernice Trousdale Nye, Prentice-Hall, 1971). An excellent supplement for rote songs with a small range is *Sing It Yourself*, which contains sections of songs with ranges of (a) a third and fourth, (b) a fifth, and (c) a sixth and seventh.

The purpose of schooling is to enable each child to learn as much as possible. Young children who do not learn number facts or letter sounds are at a real disadvantage during arithmetic and reading instruction periods. Young children who do not learn how to sing are similarly at a distinct disadvantage during subsequent years of music class. The opportunity for successful participation in singing must be given to all young children. The future of music programs should not depend on stopgap public relations, but rather on adequate and improved instruction in the most important activity in elementary music—singing.

Notes

1. Edwin Gordon, *The Psychology of Music Teaching* (Englewood Cliffs, NJ: Prentice-Hall, 1971), 272.

2. J. M. Kavanaugh, "The Development of Vocal Concepts in Children. The Methodologies Recommended in Designated Elementary Music Series" (Dissertation Abstracts International, 1983, 43, 2270-A).

3. A. Oren Gould, "Developing Specialized Programs for Singing in the Elementary School," *Bulletin of the Council for Research in Music Education*, no. 17 (1969): 9-22.

4. Emlyn Roberts and Ann D. M. Davies, "Poor Pitch Singing: Response of Monotone Singers to a Program of Remedial Training." *Journal of Research in Music Education* 23 (1975): 237-39.

5. David R. Joyner, "The Monotone Problem," *Journal of Research in Music Education* 17 (1969): 115-24.

6. Helmut Moog, "The Development of Musical Experience in Children of Pre-School Age," *Psychology of Music* 4 (1976): 38-45.

7. Graham F. Welch, "Vocal Range and Poor Pitch Singing." *Psychology of Music* 7 (1979): 13-31.

Wanted: Children to Sing and Learn

by Mary Goetze

People everywhere seem to warm to the sound of children singing. In this country, numerous children's vocal ensembles are arousing strong support and sincere artistic respect in their communities. Initially, adults may be charmed by the fact that "miniature" choristers are performing, but those who listen carefully discover that children's choirs are capable of sensitive musical performances.

The educational value of the performance experience is entirely dependent, however, on the conductor's values and skills. Traditionally, the main focus of children's choir rehearsals has been to prepare for performance, not to educate the children in music. It is common practice to learn the music in the most expedient manner and for the choristers to serve as the "subjects" of the conductor. The children usually do not participate in or even understand the reasons for artistic decisions; more often they simply carry out the conductor's instructions. In general, the process of preparing children's choirs for performance has been an occasion for little more than incidental learning. It is my belief, however, that children's choral conductors must balance the demands of

Mary Goetze is an associate professor of music at the Indiana University School of Music, Bloomington. This article originally appeared in the December 1988 Music Educators Journal.

performance with the responsibility for long-term development of the choristers.

Assessing Skills

The first step in choral music education is to thoroughly and honestly assess the independent skills and knowledge of the choir as a whole and of individual members. As a conductor, you should use entrance auditions and periodic progress evaluations to measure more than vocal quality and range; you also should consider music-reading ability, tonal memory, and independence in part-singing. It is a mistake to assess these skills while someone plays the vocal part of the piano or while you sing along: This results in an inflated notion of abilities and, in turn, perpetuates the choristers' dependency on you and the accompanist. Choristers need to be evaluated individually or in small groups. For part-singing, ask them to sing one vocal part while you or another child sings a series of short melodic and rhythmic patterns that progress from easy to difficult. Students' tonal memory can be assessed by having them echo-sing a series of patterns that increase in length and are progressively more difficult.

When you know the true music level of your choir, you can select vocal warm-ups, reading exercises, and music passages that will strengthen the choristers' deficiencies. When choosing literature, plan a strategy for presenting the material, and when determining rehearsal procedures, structure them to provide opportunities for advancing the students' skills.

Selecting Literature

When choosing music for performance you must consider the following questions: Is it appropriate for the performance? Are the musical demands commensurate with the potential of the group? What new skills can the choir learn, and what skills can be reinforced through this music? Is this music worthy of the time it will take to learn?

At first glance, it might seem that a consideration of independent skill levels would impose tight restrictions on the choice of literature. In the case of music reading, for instance, it may be necessary to choose only simple music for a choir with poor sight-singing skills. This approach, however, does not require that every section be independently learned. In a complex work of music there is inevitably a portion that can be extracted for reading experience. You can use a rhythmic or melodic pattern to practice familiar elements or to introduce an unknown one. The rest of the work can be taught by conventional methods, such as rote teaching, modeling, or accompanied reading.

Reading skills are only one aspect of music that you should consider when assessing the educational potential of the literature. You might select literature to teach dynamic markings, to practice a controlled accelerando, or to help students recognize changing or irregular meter. Other literature might provide your chorus with the opportunity to

learn about an unfamiliar style or period or to become acquainted with a particular composer.

Your literature choice also will influence the choristers' nascent musical tastes. Too often, conductors make literature choices to appease the perceived preferences of the general population, to entertain the parents, or to ensure the child's immediate acceptance of the music. Setting standards is part of your educational responsibility. Through

Figure 1. © Copyright 1967 by Boosey & Hawkes, Inc. Used by permission.

Figure 2.

Figure 3.

your choices you educate not only the children in your choirs, but the expectations of their audiences as well.

Presenting the Literature

It is your role as the conductor to build a bridge between the child and the music to be learned. Admittedly, the shortest route may be to teach the music by rote or to sing it with the choristers as they read along. Although this serves to prepare the music for performance, it will not serve your students in the future. You should build a permanent structure to provide the singers with the means to reach both the work at hand *and* the next ones with increasing independence.

Devising a strategy for introducing a work that advances skills is a musical, pedagogical, and creative process. It must begin with a thorough analysis of the music—its scale, form, rhythmic elements, text, texture, dynamics, and tempo. When planning how to introduce a work, you must consider not only these musical elements and the level of the choristers' skills, but also the types of activities that appeal to the age-group of your choir. No recipes for strategies exist because each one depends on the music and the choir. The following ex-

amples illustrate how these concepts can be used:

Example 1

Analyze the excerpt of "Long, Long Ago," arranged by Carlisle Floyd, in figure 1: It contains fairly simple rhythms, a recurring melodic pattern, and changing meters. These elements will be included in the learning process.

1. Sing the notes F, G, F, B-flat, and F, which is the melodic pattern of the first phrase of the work. The choir should echo the pattern.

2. Show the motive in melodic notation, and ask the choir to read it (see figure 2).

3. Add the correct motivic rhythm to the pitches. First, ask the choir members to clap the rhythm, then think the pitches while you clap the rhythm. Second, ask them to sing the pattern.

4. Show a different rhythm to the choir (see figure 3), and repeat the procedure in step three. This prepares them for the various forms of the patterns in the music and expands their ability to coordinate the readings of pitch and rhythm.

5. Hand out the music. The singers should discover how many times the pattern occurs in the soprano part of the first section. They should also read the text that accompanies each pattern. Then have the choir sing the patterns with the text.

Figure 4.

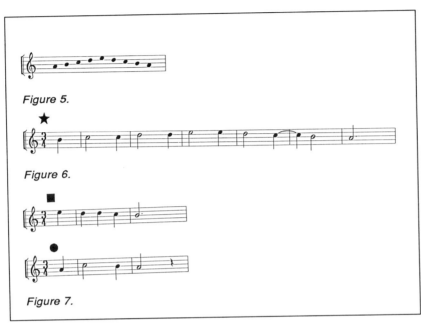

Figure 5.

Figure 6.

Figure 7.

6. Have the choir sing the pattern each time it occurs (as they read the score) as you sing all of the other measures; this method gives the singers a feeling for the entire melody of the A section. (They will be learning the remainder of the melody by using the rote method.)

7. Repeat step 6 with accompaniment.

8. Sing the work again, and have the choristers sing the motive while counting the beats and conducting during the measures you sing. They should discover the changing meter of the work.

9. Have the choir sing the entire soprano part of the A section. (The alto part will be learned similarly in a later rehearsal.)

Example 2

When presenting "Alleluja" from *Cantata No. 142*, attributed to Johann Sebastian Bach (see figure 4), have the choristers sight-read the three different phrases in the melody line (this work is arranged for two voices, but only the melody line is shown here). After listening to the entire work, they will identify the order of the phrases and the duration of the rests between them.

1. Have the choir echo-sing a pentachord in A minor (see figure 5). Sing it from low to high, then from low to high to low. Write the pentachord on the board.

2. Rewrite the pattern to become the third phrase of the work (see figure 6); the choir should then identify the changes that have been made. Have the choir sing the phrase as you supply the rhythm by pointing to the notes in time.

3. Add the patterns in figure 7, and sight-read them in a similar manner. Label the patterns in figures 6 and 7 with shapes such as squares or circles.

4. Have the singers determine the order of the phrases as they listen to the first four phrases with accompaniment.

5. Once the choir has determined the correct order of the phrases, substitute letter names for the shapes. The choir should identify the form of the work as AABC.

6. Add the text "Alleluja" to the A phrases. Teach students to use proper phrasing, vowel sounds, and accents. Have students sing this phrase as it occurs in the work, and listen to the entire work to determine the form. They should discover that the form is AABCBBC.

7. Have the singers count the number of downbeats before, between, and after the phrases. Hand out the music so they can check their answers against the score.

8. Repeat step seven as each student watches his or her copy of the music.

9. In subsequent rehearsals, introduce the B and C phrases with the text. Teach the harmony line, using similar techniques.

This type of approach engages the choristers in the learning process so deeply that they do not have a chance to reject the work. Because children are much less likely to "turn off" to music they know, this process gives them the opportunity to learn the music intimately before they think about whether they like it. Having made this intellectual investment in the music, they are far less apt to dislike it.

Refining the Performance

Once the music is learned there are still opportunities to nurture the children's artistic sensitivity. You can do this by including them in the artistic process of refinement. Conductors make artistic decisions based on the sounds they hear; the process of shaping the performance of music is guided by the conductor's perception of his or her ensemble. The conductor need not be the only artist in the choir, however. You should guide choristers to perceive their own sound (that is, listen to themselves and others), and you should also involve them in refining and therefore controlling production of that sound. In this manner, you can teach children to behave as artists. The following are two ways to apply this idea in rehearsals:

To bring attention to the target phrase, provide a "mirror" of the sound of the choir. Sing a phrase as an example but with an error, such as an out-of-tune pitch, an incorrect vowel sound, or an imprecise rhythm; then ask the choir to describe what was wrong and to propose a solution. Direct the children's suggestions toward ideas that will produce the musical shape you prefer.

Another procedure is to sing the problem phrase incorrectly and then correctly. Ask the children to choose the better performance, and then have them imitate it. In both of these examples the correction is achieved as effectively as in conventional verbalizing or modeling. With this approach, however, they are learning to monitor and to correct their own contributions to the choral sound and are involved in making discriminations that lead to the independent evaluation of their own performances.

Selecting the Choristers

Traditionally, children's choirs have served only a small, select number of children. Music educators must make the richly educational choral experience available to more than a chosen few. This proposal has several important implications. First, it suggests that children's choruses should become a vital part of elementary schools, communities, universities, and places of worship. Ideally, school choirs should have rehearsals during the school day rather than before or after school or during recesses. In addition, this proposal supports the formation of community-based programs that are accessible to all, both in terms of cost and location. If needed, donations or scholarships can help those who cannot afford to join.

Second, children's choirs should be available to all students who express an interest in singing, regardless of their musical or vocal gifts. Auditions should not serve as the basis for elimination, but rather for placement. On the other hand, children should not be required to participate in choral programs. The captive choir member rarely contributes to the general esprit de corps and will probably not reap the aesthetic and educational benefits of the experience.

Participating in a choir can have a profound effect on the musical development of young singers. Children can receive a truly *musical* education as they prepare for performance. Through firsthand experience, children can learn melody, rhythm, and form as they sing. Ideally, choristers will participate in shaping and refining the music and, at the same time, respond to it aesthetically. When these experiences are paired with the extramusical benefits of the choral experience (such as praise from their family and the public) and the social interaction with other children who share their interest in music, young singers can embark on lifetimes of making music.

Let the Whole School Sing !

by Nell J. Sins

A group of French medical students sings folk songs in the courtyard of their university until all hours of the night. Spanish teenagers in a park improvise vocal numbers accompanied by complicated clapping rhythms. This type of spontaneous group singing is familiar to anyone who has spent time in a foreign county. In contrast, many Americans are extremely self-conscious about public singing. How can American music educators help their students overcome this fear? First, they must provide students with experiences that contribute to a feeling of naturalness in group singing. An all-school sing at the elementary level can provide this type of rewarding experience for students and teachers alike.

Of course, students must learn songs in small groups before they are able to participate in an all-school sing, but what happens next? Your first task is to sell the idea of such an assembly to your principal and to fellow teachers. Your "sales pitch" will be enhanced if the songs to be used are related to other school projects or are associated culturally with the surrounding community.

Teachers must be made aware of the fact that the very first song assembly will be so new and different to students that there may be some disci-pline problems. Assure your colleagues that, as the children overcome their self-consciousness and get swept up in the joy of singing, inappropriate behavior will all but disappear.

You will probably want the first few assemblies to be divided into lower grades (K–3) and upper grades (4–6). For each level, make a list of songs that you consider appropriate for large-group singing.

In a large-group setting, very young children will listen to and enjoy the music at first, then join in when they are ready. The K–3 group will enjoy call-and-response songs, story songs, and simple folk songs. At any level, you can make a sing a multimedia event by showing slides made from pictures drawn in the classroom.

In the beginning, so that you can adapt tempos as needed, plan to accompany all songs yourself on piano, guitar, or Autoharp, using amplification if necessary. When a large group sings call-and-response songs, it is often effective to have the teacher sing the "call" and the entire group sing the "response" portion. Very young children, however, sometimes take such pride in the fact that they know the entire song that they will sing both the call *and* the response. When this occurs, it is time to divide the entire student body into half "call" and half "response." The children will want to switch off from time to time.

For the upper elementary level, seasonal songs are appropriate, as are patriotic songs and an occasional popular song. Try simple rounds that you

Nell Sins is a professor of music education at the University of South Carolina in Columbia. This article originally appeared in the January 1990 Music Educators Journal.

have tested in the classroom. Actually, rounds sometimes work better in large groups than in small ones because the students can hear their parts better. Cumulative songs are also fun.

Your goal is to bring the entire school together when you believe the students are ready. As you go along in smaller-group song sessions, evaluate the songs and their successes, and determine what songs might be used for the large assembly. You might also have one group sing their songs for the other group.

You, the music teacher, will emcee the programs for all the singing assemblies. Be sure to include many enthusiastic comments: "Wow, that was great! Thanks for singing 'The Erie Canal' with such enthusiasm. Our media specialist, Ms. Smith, has a wonderful book about the Erie Canal with lots of pictures. She's going to display it out on the main table in the media center so you can all see what life was like on a canal boat."

Do all-school sings work? You will receive an answer later in the year when you find yourself on a field-trip bus and students spontaneously break into song, then go from one song to the next. At that point, you can start asking, "What songs can we all sing together *next* year?"

LISTENING

Active involvement while listening to music is an important goal of elementary instruction. Because music moves through time, it is more difficult to focus and sustain young listeners by means of verbal directions alone. The articles on listening contain varied and effective ways to actively involve children in this important activity.

Creative listening strategies based on the divergent production abilities of fluency, flexibility, and elaboration constitute one approach to the involvement of listeners throughout a piece of music. Listening maps and call charts are instructional devices that can be created for any piece of music. Each device provides a visual guide to direct perceptive listening. Even though the music examples in each article cited are limited to the Western art-music tradition, the techniques are adaptable to any style of music.

Creative Problem-Solving and the Music Listening Experience

by Saul Feinberg

The one learning experience that best reflects the significant changes that have occurred in music education over the past decade is listening. Taken out of the passive, rather perfunctory role it played in former days, listening has been elevated to a position where its true function in music and general education can at last be realized. This function, essentially, is to serve as a means by which all individuals can respond aesthetically to what is expressive in music.

Such conferences as the Yale seminar in Music Education, the Tanglewood Symposium, the institutes for the Contemporary Music Project, and more recently, the Conference for Advanced Placement in Music have consistently emphasized the importance of listening courses in helping both the performer and the nonperformer deal more perceptively and affectively with music. They have also

Saul Feinberg teaches music at Lincoln High School, Philadelphia, Pennsylvania. This article originally appeared in the September 1974 Music Educators Journal.

called for approaches that can make these learning experiences more dynamic and more creative. Paradoxically, however, while the purposes and values of aesthetically oriented courses in music have been dealt with in deep and penetrating ways, the means by which these goals can actually be realized in the classroom have been given only minimal attention by the profession.

A Multifaceted Approach

The reasons for this gap between the philosophy and the practices of aesthetic education become clear when we realize that many music educators are still using rather limited strategies and activities to deal with one of humanity's most complex and revealing phenomena—the aesthetic experience. These approaches include those that emphasize the programmatic, nonmusical aspects of music and those that concentrate too much on the factual content of music. What is needed is an approach to aesthetic listening that not only enables students to learn *about* music but also encourages them to respond intellectually and affectively to the creative process that produced it. Such a multifaceted approach—an approach that is close to both the creative process and the created product (the music)—can be properly called a "creative problem-solving approach."

Essentially, a creative approach to perceptive listening involves the setting up of problem-solving situations in which the listener can function as both a thinker (a problem-solver) and a learner (a gainer of knowledge). In such a setting, the students are not told what is significant in a piece of music, nor are they informed as to what is happening in the work. Rather, they are given opportunities to explore these possibilities for themselves by working out various problems and hypotheses. Such an analytical approach enables students to think in the manner of a composer as well as a listener. In such roles, they are able to share some of the problems faced by the composer and to respond to the work's aesthetic qualities in a deep and penetrating way.

A creative problem-solving approach can do more than merely teach content. While students are learning fundamental ideas about music, they can also cultivate those behaviors of thinking and listening that will promote a pattern of continuous aesthetic and creative growth. Certainly, such a product as this represents the ultimate goal of all aesthetic music education programs.

If this creative approach is based on the belief that students can develop intellectual abilities at the same time they are acquiring knowledge, the question can be asked, "What abilities?" Fortunately, answers to this question have come out of the extensive research that has taken place over the past two decades in the area of creative behavior. So revealing have the results of this research been that they have implications not only for disciplines naturally linked with the creative process—such as those in art education—but for all the subject areas in general education.

A Look at Human Intelligence

Of central importance have been the changing beliefs about the nature and nurturing of creative potential. In sharp contrast to the earlier viewpoint that creativeness is a quality reserved only for the gifted few, today it is seen as a quality that all individuals possess in some degree—a quality that each person has the democratic right and the psychological need to develop. Through the pioneering efforts of such creative psychologists as J. P. Guilford, P. R. Merrifield, and E. Paul Torrance, specific behaviors of problem-solving and creative thinking have been delineated that can be significantly improved when appropriate conditions for their development are made available. Most of these creative-thinking abilities have been identified from the extensive studies with Guilford's extraordinary model of human intelligence, the structure-of-intellect model. In this model, Guilford and his associates have been able to hypothesize 120 intellectual abilities, each of which has its own distinctive quality. Ninety-eight of these abilities have already been demonstrated through a complex system of factor analysis.[1]

Although it is conceivable that all the intellectual abilities theorized in the structure-of-intellect model could be dealt with in some way in a creative listening approach, the abilities most compatible with such an approach are those classified under the operation labeled "divergent production." In contrast to the other thinking processes in the model, this operation is concerned with generating solutions to a problem that are both useful and innovative. Since divergent production involves the bringing together of previously unrelated ideas to arrive at a solution, it is the cognitive process most identified with creative thinking. The "divergent thinking" abilities most important for a creative approach to perceptive music listening are fluency, flexibility, and elaboration.

In terms of general intellectual functioning, fluency is concerned with the ability to generate a quantity of adaptable (but not necessarily original) solutions to a problem within a certain amount of time. In many tests for fluent thinking, the individual is asked to describe as many uses as possible for a particular object—for example, a hammer. The more solutions the individual is able to produce, the higher the fluency score would be. This ability can be related to perceptive music listening by asking the listener to tell how many different ways a particular musical idea is used in a given piece of music. The more uses perceived, the more fluent the listening. The following section of this article includes several examples of listening tasks that require fluent thinking abilities (suggestions for specific compositions or ideas that can be used are enclosed in brackets).

Some Listening Tasks

1. Before listening to the following music example [the opening section from Schubert's *Symphony No. 5* in B-flat], describe the different ways you think the main motif could be used in the music.

2. Three different themes will be played for you. After listening to them, pick out two that you think were written by the same composer, and explain how they are related.

3. I will play two themes for you. If you were asked to compose a bridge connecting these two themes, how would you organize such a passage?

Flexibility, as a divergent thinking behavior, is concerned with generating many different kinds of logical solutions to a problem. Although this behavior is closely linked with fluency, it is involved more with how many changes or alternative means were used to solve the problem than with the quantity of responses. Flexibility implies openness and originality. In terms of perceptive music listening, flexibility involves tasks that ask the listener to indicate the different ways in which musical ideas are changed and combined in a piece of music. The more fixated the listener is on any one element in the music, such as rhythm, the less he or she is able to respond as a flexible listener. Here are three examples of listening tasks that call for flexible thinking:

1. After listening to the following composition ["Chester" from William Schuman's *New England Triptych*], make up a series of questions that you think relate to what you heard. Remember, the

more areas you touch on in your questions, the more flexibly you are thinking.

2. While listening to the following work [the second movement of Paul Hindemith's *Symphonic Metamorphosis of Themes by Weber*], place a check after any of the music qualities listed on your "Aural Flexibility List" (see figure 1) whenever they reappear in the music. Each section will be indicated to you. Don't get stuck on any one quality.

3. After listening to two different recordings of the same composition [the finale from Béla Bartók's *Concerto for Orchestra*], describe what you think the second conductor did that was different from what the first conductor did. Which version did you find more satisfying? Why?

Elaboration is the creative thinking behavior concerned with generating step-by-step procedures to solve a particular problem. Again, the more useful and original the solution, the more creative is the thinking expressed. Relating elaborative thinking to perceptive music listening involves tasks in which the listener indicates procedures needed to carry out various ideas through music. Here are two examples:

1. Listen to the music up to ... [the gong at the end of Peter Ilyich Tchaikovsky's *Symphony No. 2* in C minor ("Little Russian")]. Keeping in mind what you have heard, describe how you would bring this work to an end.

2. Refer to your "Music Qualities List" (see figure 2), and write down the numbers of those qualities you think could be used to depict each of the following scenes [an approaching storm, the storm itself, the end of the storm]. While listening to this selection [the fourth movement from Ludwig van Beethoven's *Symphony No. 6* in F major], circle the number of those qualities that were used by the composer to give an impression in music of these scenes. (This type of musical "Bingo" activity could be adapted to numerous other elaborative listening tasks concerned with describing various music forms and contemporary styles.)

Stages of Creative Thinking

Considering the complexity of creative thinking and the multiplicity of ways to approach creative

Music Qualities	Sections in the Music									
	1	2	3	4	5	6	7	8	9	10
a change in tempo										
a melody in low register										
melody against melody										
thick, dissonant chords										
a crescendo										
a sudden change in volume										
a solo wind instrument										
a percussion instrument										
pizzicato										
a new theme										
a return to the "A" theme										
a question-answer effect										
number of qualities heard										

Total

Figure 1. Aural Flexibility List

teaching, you could easily wonder how it is possible to translate all these factors into a program of meaningful teaching-learning experiences. Once again, however, a solution to the problem can be found in the results of research into creative behavior. A model for structuring a creative problem-solving approach can be identified in the very process of creative thinking itself. This process has been described in many different ways by many different scholars. All these diversified descriptions, however, tend to hypothesize the creative-thinking process as consisting of three interrelated stages—a *preparational stage* in which a problem is perceived, identified, and prepared for some kind of solution (problem-solving activity cannot occur until a gap

in information is sensed by the individual); an *exploratory-transformative stage* in which possible answers to the problem are explored and gradually transformed into some kind of solution (the longer the search is sustained, the richer and more creative the solution is likely to be); and a *synthetic stage* in which the solution is evaluated and internalized for future learning tasks (the ultimate result being further learning and growth for the individual).

This preparational–exploratory-transformative–synthetic sequence of problem solving can serve as a model for many different experiences in a music listening course. It can be used to structure individual lessons, to unify several different lessons, or to organize a series of interrelated lessons made up of listening episodes. What is basically involved in all these structures is a series of preparational activities in which specific problems relating to a music idea or a specific work of music can be identified, a series of exploratory-transformative activities in which many different kinds of solutions can be generated through creative problem-solving experiences with the elements and the processes of the music being explored (it is in this stage that all of the divergent thinking abilities described earlier could be used), and a series of synthetic activities in which understandings and skills learned from the problem-solving experience can become internalized and applied to new listening tasks.

It is interesting to realize not only that the tripartite design of creative thinking is an appropriate model for organizing the lessons of a listening episode, but also that it can serve as a means by which the entire listening course can be structured. Such a plan would consist of three developmental phases—a preparational phase, an exploratory-transformative phase, and a synthetic phase.

In the preparational phase of the course, the prime objective is to establish a level of openness and flexibility on the part of students that will enable them to cope with increasingly complex and

RHYTHM	1.	Steady pulse	DYNAMICS	23.	Gradually louder
	2.	Irregular pulse		24.	Gradually softer
	3.	No pulse		25.	Suddenly loud
	4.	Generally slow tempo		26.	Suddenly soft
	5.	Generally fast tempo		27.	Many dynamic changes
	6.	Gradually slower		28.	Few dynamic changes—generally soft
	7.	Gradually faster		29.	Few dynamic changes—generally loud
	8.	A sudden change in tempo	TONE COLOR	30.	Solo tone colors
MELODY	9.	Generally a stepwise melody		31.	Small performance group (fewer than fifteen)
	10.	A very jumpy melody		32.	Large performance group (more than fifteen)
	11.	A simple, songlike melody			
	12.	A very elaborate melody		33.	Electronic sounds
	13.	Melodic ornaments (trills, mordents)		34.	Pizzicato effects
HARMONY	14.	Generally traditional harmonies		35.	Cymbal crash
	15.	Many dissonant harmonies		36.	Drum rolls
	16.	A "key" feeling (tonal)		37.	Traditional tone colors
	17.	No feeling of "key" (atonal)		38.	Unusual tone colors
	18.	Shifting "key" feeling (modulation)		39.	Very high or low registers
	19.	Same texture throughout—generally thin	FORM	40.	Balanced ideas
				41.	Many repeated ideas
	20.	Same texture throughout—generally thick		42.	Question-answer effect
				43.	Only one section
	21.	Homophonic texture (melody against chords)		44.	Two or more sections (or themes)
	22.	Polyphonic texture (melody against melody)		45.	"Freely" organized

Figure 2. Music Qualities List

sophisticated kinds of listening tasks. This phase of the course is particularly important because its purpose is to formulate an attitudinal frame of reference that is sufficiently divergent to sustain a pattern of continuous learning throughout the course (and perhaps, beyond). From the various lessons in the preparational phase, students can learn the following basic guidelines for becoming more perceptive music listeners:

- Try to give your full attention to the music being heard.
- Focus on the various elements that make up the music.
- Be open to new listening experiences, not "blinded" by past listening habits.
- Postpone your judgment of the music until it has been fully experienced.
- Listen to the music many times.

An example of a preparational listening lesson structured along the lines of the creative-thinking model is described in figure 3.

In the exploratory-transformative phase of the course, the behaviors of perceptive music listening and creative problem-solving gradually merge into a totally integrated process. The primary objective of the listening episodes in this phase is to develop students' listening abilities and understandings through direct and prolonged encounters with complete works of music. Although survey lessons can be used to develop various music concepts and skills, the approach most compatible with the highly integrated nature of creative thinking is one that encourages the listener to become involved with the music elements and processes of *complete* pieces of music.

When such an approach is taken, it is possible for the listener not only to share some of the creative problems that the composer faced when writing the work, but also to experience the work as a complete, integrated whole. It is through this bringing together of the various parts previously explored that a type of musical gestalt can occur, and a more revealing aesthetic experience can take place. The dynamics of such an "aesthetic whole" approach have been described eloquently by Edmund Feldman:

The final meaning and the entire funding of meaning does not take place until the work of art has been experienced in its fullness and entirety. Until then, the perceptions are separate and the meanings provisional. Not until the whole work is experienced can the interactions among the parts take place, the sense of wholeness be achieved, and the heightening and intensification of perception be felt. [2]

Although there is a definite need for more listening materials that can help students interact more perceptively and creatively with complete works of music, several student-oriented materials have been developed. These include those by Bennett Reimer, [3] by the Yale Music Curriculum Project, [4] and by me. [5]

In the culminating phase of the course, the synthetic phase, students are given opportunities to integrate their listening behaviors and understandings by applying them to tasks that call for responses that involve synthesizing. In this stage of perceptive music listening development, students are encouraged to make aesthetic judgments when verbalizing about creative processes in music, when offering criticisms about specific works and performance interpretations, when distinguishing works that are banal from those that demonstrate creativity, and when formulating original listening guides and analyses of works of music. From these final, evaluative experiences, students should come to realize that the listening experience symbolizes a unique encounter with the human condition, an experience that grows and deepens as individuals themselves grow and deepen.

Although the main objective of this article has been to describe an approach to music listening that can bring a greater compatibility between the goals and practices of aesthetic education, there has been a larger intent as well. This is to emphasize once again that music is not just an entertaining thing to have around when "important" things are finished. It can also make a unique and significant contribution to one of general education's most valued goals—helping each person become all he or she can be, a fully thinking, knowing, and feeling individual.

A Preparational Listening Lesson

Problem: To have the students realize the importance of being open and flexible when listening to music.

Preparational activities:
Familiarize the class with the following motif (from the third movement of Bartók's *Music for Strings, Percussion, and Celesta)*:

Play a recording of the music and ask the class to listen for the motif.
Have the individual students describe what they heard. Make note of some of the ideas they may have missed, such as the motif being repeated more than ten times; the motif being played backwards (retrograde); the motif being repeated twice as fast and twice as slow (diminution and augmentation); and the motif being played as a question-answer effect.
Ask the class why they did not detect all of these ideas. Lead to the realization that most of the students were unable to recognize these things (and others) in the music because they were limiting their *listening* to only the general sounds of the orchestra.

Exploratory-transformative activities:
Emphasize the necessity of going beyond what is obvious or familiar by giving the students a divergent-thinking problem to solve, such as the following:

How many squares do you see? (By shifting one's perceptions, it is possible to count thirty squares of varying sizes.)

Replay the Bartók example to give students an opportunity to listen more divergently this time. Ask the class to indicate other qualities they were able to perceive in the music. Replay the example to amplify the responses.

Synthetic activities:
Apply the realizations about "divergent listening" by having the class describe what they hear in another work (the third movement from Brahms' *Symphony No. 4* in E minor, Op. 98).
Pose such "test" questions as these: Who can clap the rhythm of the main motif? Who can hum it? Who can play it on the piano? How many times was it repeated? How was it changed (inverted, played in a low register, played pizzicato, played in minor, and so on)?
Reemphasize the idea that the perceptive music listener is one who is open and flexible in his or her listening.

Figure 3.

Notes

1. A comprehensive discussion of this model and its three-dimensional design can be found in J. P. Guilford's *The Nature of Human Intelligence* (New York: McGraw-Hill Book Co., 1987) and in Guilford and Ralph Hoepfner's *The Analysis of Intelligence* (New York: McGraw-Hill Book Co., 1971).

2. Edmund B. Feldman, "The Nature of the Aesthetic Experience," in *Report of the Commission on Art Education*, edited by Jerome J. Hausman (Washington, DC: National Art Education Association, 1965), p. 36.

3. Bennett Reimer, *Development and Trial in a Junior and Senior High School of a Two-Year Curriculum in General Music*, Project No. H-116 (Washington, DC: U.S. Office of Education, 1967).

4. Kenneth A. Wendrick and Claude V. Palisca, *An Approach to Musical Understanding for Secondary School Students, Report of the Yale Music Curriculum Project*, Project No. 221, U.S. Office of Education (New Haven, CT: Yale University, 1970).

5. Saul Feinberg, *Blueprints for Musical Understanding*, Four Series (New York: Warner Bros. Publications, Inc., 1964, 1971).

Call Charts: Tools from the Past for Today's Classroom

by Beverly Bletstein

T eaching musical concepts to students with limited or no musical background is often a frustrating experience. We expose our students to a new language with a process that often begins with mastery of the musical alphabet. Although reading notation is a vital component of music instruction, it is equally important that students develop aural skills. Notation is merely a visual representation of musical sounds; therefore, the aural experience should serve as a prerequisite to developing a music vocabulary. Students will benefit from a variety of well-organized listening activities that clarify musical concepts. Given that the development of listening skills is of the utmost importance for successful musical learning to occur, our next task as music educators is to determine the best methods to achieve this goal.

In many instances, listening experiences are tedious for the teacher as well as the student. Additional resources facilitate the learning process and increase the students' chances for success. The use of new materials, however, does not necessarily preclude the continuation of preexisting methods.

Beverly Bletstein is an assistant professor of music education at The Ohio State University at Lima. This article was originally published in the September 1987 Music Educators Journal.

We sometimes forget (in an effort to make a lesson appealing to the students) that many techniques have survived the test of time because students have continued to succeed. One such method of aural instruction requires the use of call charts—written or visual guides that identify and define aural stimuli. As the student listens to the musical selection, the teacher announces numbers or "calls" that coincide with each musical event as it is heard. A call chart can be used to introduce new concepts or to reinforce and review previous listening lessons. Call charts have proven to be a valuable learning tool at all levels of music instruction and for all types of students. Their use has extended beyond the public school into the college curriculum and has been helpful to both music and nonmusic majors.

Adding a Visual Element

The most obvious reason for student achievement is that the call chart provides a visual element in an area of learning that normally is abstract. When the musical sounds are no longer present, the student often is called upon to identify the aural elements, using the appropriate terminology. This requires memory skills that the student may not have yet developed. Since the call chart is a written reference guide, it allows the student to refer back to a particular listening experience and recall specific elements of the example. Its value extends beyond the realm of retention skills. The call chart focuses the student's attention on the listening task. One of the most difficult musical skills to master is that of concentrated listening. Students find an abstract skill like music listening more useable when it is put into a concrete, written format.

Although call charts have proven to be an effective instructional tool for music and classroom teachers, they also have proven to be an aid to independent study. Listening skills cannot be developed in the classroom alone. Continued listening experiences must become a part of the learner's daily routine. Assignments are enhanced through the use of call charts that are specifically designed to assist the beginning listener as he or she attempts to work independently. The call chart increases the probability that students will experience some success when the instructor is not present.

Finally, call charts can be used in the evaluation process by teachers and students. Each call chart can be designed to elicit written responses. Two ways in which a written response can be obtained are: (1) inserting sections in the call chart that ask students to identify repetitive listening events, such as the recurrence of a particular theme and (2) providing lists of questions to accompany the call chart that focus on the specific musical elements the student is expected to identify. The students do not have to wait for an evaluation—the teacher can correct their responses immediately following the listening activity. More important, the teacher may design listening assignments that enable students to process and evaluate aural stimuli with greater ease outside the classroom. Pretaped

musical selections with verbal calls will increase students' ability to follow a chart independently. As a result, they are able to review musical concepts presented previously by the teacher. In addition, the teacher may find that many students are capable of hearing new musical elements independently when given carefully prepared charts and tapes.

Developing Call Charts

Constructing call charts requires careful consideration. Many variables determine the effectiveness of the final product. Devise a systematic plan for preparing the charts to ensure the validity of the content. The outline that follows will help the novice become familiar with call chart construction:

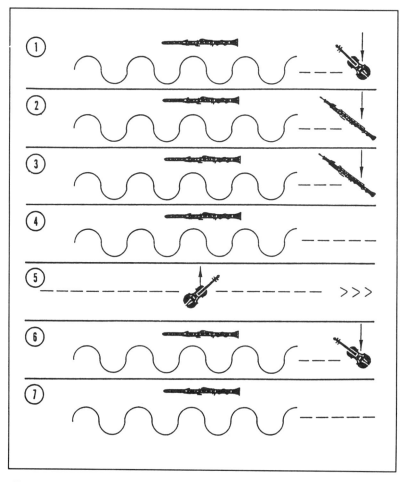

Figure 1.

1. Identify the student population for which the call chart is designed. Call charts are ideal for use with elementary, secondary, and college students. The level of difficulty of the call chart will depend on the students' age and musical development. Simplified versions that require limited writing and rely on graphic designs or pictures are preferred for the young child (see figure 1). Excessive use of complete sentences and complex terminology that is beyond the students' comprehension can distract them from the listening task.

2. Limit the number of new concepts introduced in each chart. The call chart in figure 1 is an example for teaching melodic contour; the musical selection is short, and the student is given only a visual representation of the direction of the melody.

one or two primary musical concepts at any given time.

3. Design the call chart to introduce new concepts or review concepts previously learned. Do not try to cover too much material in one lesson, especially if the students are inexperienced listeners. (This is also true when working with more advanced students.) It is often wise to stay within the prescribed characteristics of the chosen musical element (for example, melody), although a limited number of musical elements may be combined within the same call chart (for example, rhythm and melody). This is an acceptable and valid use of the chart if its design coincides with the musical development of the students. Figure 2 reviews the concept of melodic contour, introduces students to the string technique known as pizzicato, and shows the rhythmic and melodic use of the ostinato. The teacher should be aware that the written notation of the ostinato is included only when the students have mastered reading simple notation in 4/4 time.

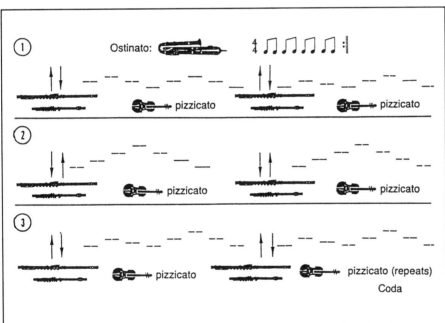

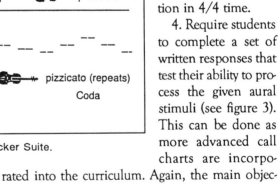

Figure 2. Call chart for "Chinese Dance" from The Nutcracker Suite.

4. Require students to complete a set of written responses that test their ability to process the given aural stimuli (see figure 3). This can be done as more advanced call charts are incorporated into the curriculum. Again, the main objective of this call chart is to teach melodic contour.

Pictures of the instruments playing the melody and melodic extensions introduce the element of tone color as a secondary concept. When the students' reading ability permits, the teacher may include the written names of the instruments on the call chart. Young children are not capable of processing several different aural stimuli at once, so it is best to concentrate on

The chart in figure 3 is more complex than the charts in figures 1 and 2. The terms *tremolo*, *glissando*, *fanfare*, *crescendo*, and *chord* have been added for more advanced students at the upper elementary or secondary level. These, however, can easily be eliminated from the chart for use with younger children. Students are then asked to identify the instrument playing the fanfare and also the melodic contour. The instructor may prefer to provide students with a list of questions following the lesson. The advantage of this option is that the student can respond without having to keep pace with the music; the disadvantage is made obvious when the student attempts to recall the specific events when the aural stimulus is no longer present. Whenever possible, it is preferable to include the written responses in the call chart. As students listen to the musical selection, their perceptions of the devices used remain fresh in their minds. To alleviate the problem of responding and listening simultaneously, the teacher should be careful to limit the number of sections on the chart that require a response and be sure to alternate these with portions specifically designed for listening only.

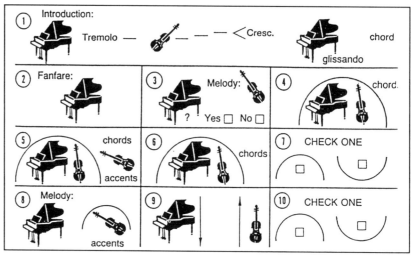

Figure 3. Call chart for "Royal March of the Lion" from Carnival of the Animals

5. Print or type call charts, and divide each call so the student can identify each charted musical event clearly. Cluttered charts are difficult to read and add to the complexity of the listening lesson. Young children need to see pictures and large words with adequate space between items. This can be achieved by dividing the paper into numbered boxes, with one box for each call. Advanced students at the secondary and college level can use call charts with more verbal information and fewer visual aids.

6. Develop additional charts to reinforce the same concept. The charts in figures 1, 2, and 3 were designed to teach melodic contour. Repetition enhances learning. It is dangerous to assume that students will master the art of listening or a specific musical concept in a few class periods.

7. Use the same musical composition to teach different concepts. As students become familiar with the musical example, they become ready to focus their attention on other devices in the piece. Consequently, they come to realize the multifaceted qualities of a composition and the ways that each musical element enhances the character of the entire work.

Advanced Call Charts

Call charts can be a positive addition to the college curriculum. Teachers have long been aware of the value of visual aids in the learning process. College-age students are not too old to experience the positive effects of a visual learning tool if it helps them succeed. An advanced call chart is a challenge both for the teacher to construct and the student to master. Due to their ability to process more information, college students often comprehend more complex musical events. This gives the instructor a wider range of musical literature from which to select listening examples. Longer examples can be included, such as overtures and movements from symphonies, sonatas, and concertos. The key to the student's success will be the ability of the teacher to assess his or her students accurately. A listening lesson can be either too simple or too complex for a group of students if their musical development has been evaluated incorrectly.

The call chart shown in figure 4 is designed for the more advanced student. As in figures 1, 2, and 3, this chart is designed to teach melodic contour.

The names of the instruments in figure 4 may be substituted for the pictures, although visual aids often enhance learning for older or advanced students (especially nonmusic majors). Other musical elements are included in this example, many of which are related to the melodic characteristics of the piece. Some of the concepts presented here have been previously introduced to the students and are in the call chart as a review. Students can complete a call chart like the one in figure 4 when all the proper prerequisites have been met. The teacher must prepare the students for this chart by providing isolated examples of tone color, sequence, conjunct and disjunct melodies, cadences, and themes.

The responsibility for developing listening skills must be shared by both teachers and students. The proper use of call charts will increase the probability that students will master listening and listening-related tasks. As music educators, we must be the ones to promote good listening habits as well as a positive and healthy attitude about music at all levels of instruction. The call chart is one device that can help us achieve this goal.

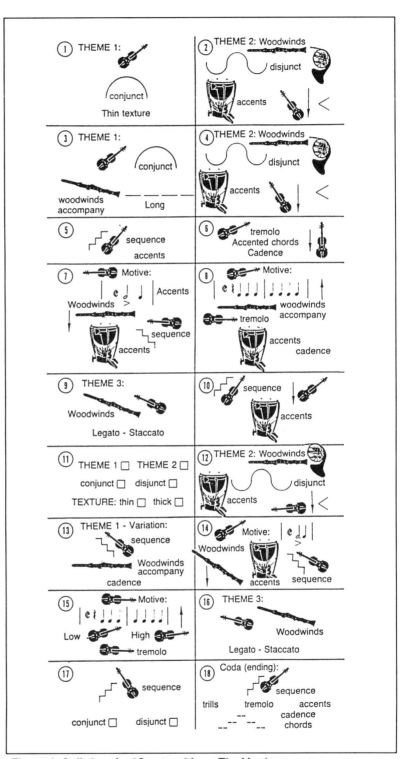

Figure 4. Call chart for "Overture" from The Marriage of Figaro

Listening Maps for Musical Tours

by Samuel D. Miller

A "listening map" is a graphic representation that symbolizes the essential features of a musical selection in a visual format. The map may be quite creative and intricate, involving pictures, colors, abstract designs, and geometric forms—or it may be quite simple, involving two or three basic symbols. It is a valuable teaching aid for the music-listening lesson because it visually represents exactly where musical events take place, making it easier for children to understand musical relationships, especially regarding balance and contrast. In addition to containing elements related to form, the listening map may also illustrate features related to melody, dynamics, instrumentation, and aspects of rhythm.

Probably the most valuable type of listening map is one created by the children themselves through teacher guidance. The process is stimulating and interesting to children, prompting attentive listening, lively discussions, analytical thought processes, and creativity. The main objective is to develop a map that presents the most important "clues" to the music at hand, yet one that is simple, clear, and direct.

Once a good map is developed—on a chalkboard, feltboard, or large tablet—it can be transferred easily to a permanent chart, transparency, or

Samuel D. Miller is a professor of music education at the University of Houston, Texas. This article originally appeared in the October 1986 Music Educators Journal.

a ditto master, making it possible for each child to own a personal copy. Over the years, teachers can build a sizeable, ready repertory of listening maps that can contribute greatly to the overall music listening program and cut down tremendously on class preparation time. These maps can be used in conjunction with singing, instrumental playing, creative movement, and dramatization—all of which are typically incorporated within or related to the listening program.

Theme Notation

Music selections in the general music class are frequently familiarized and studied through singing themes. Perhaps this is the most direct way for children to internalize selections. Since in most music the themes signal the important points of arrival and change, it seems appropriate that their notation, either in conventional or graphic notation, be presented as part of the listening map itself or in conjunction with it during the lesson. Melodic materials will prove to be especially useful for teachers who emphasize solfège singing according to the principles of Kodály or mallet instrument playing according to Orff. Moreover, teachers fluent at the piano or on another instrument will be able to play the themes and bring a personal touch to the lessons. For these reasons, all of the significant themes, both initial and internal, should be sought out and presented.

A listening map that illustrates the essential features and themes of a selection provides the *frame-*

work for developing an interesting and informative listening lesson. It is not the end product in itself; rather, it facilitates bringing music listening to children in a personalized, exciting way. Undoubtedly, discussions, classroom activities such as rhythmic dramatization or musical performance, and quiet reflection will lead to much more, so that the total listening experience is multidimensional.

Listening Map Examples

Let us turn our attention to four rather simple listening maps that "tell" much about the music they represent. Although the selections are presented in order of complexity of concepts to be taught, all of these can be used to advantage even with very young listeners. For example, the fourth one, Stravinsky's "Berceuse" from *The Firebird*, was designed by an elementary music teacher who first tried it on her seven-year-old son.[1] While at first glance the map may appear to be complex, she reports that he caught its significance immediately and insisted on "pointing" his way through the piece repeatedly. Later, she enthusiastically reported success in teaching the work to her elementary classes.

"Bydlo" from *Pictures at an Exhibition* (Modest Mussorgsky)—a low-pitched piece with a steady, laborious eighth-note accompaniment throughout and a hauntingly beautiful melody introduced by the tuba, this work is a perennial favorite with children.

The map (figure 1) indicates several important things about this Russian work. The melody suggests a simple song sung by an oxcart driver to the steady pounding of hoofbeats. The duple-metered rhythmic accompaniment is continuous throughout and is represented by the alternating heavy and light vertical bar lines. In terms of dynamics, the selection begins softly, as if the cart is off in the distance, then gradually becomes thunderously loud

as the cart draws closer to the observer, finally fading away to nothing. This musical episode is represented not only by the roadway in the picture itself but also by the dynamic markings underneath.

Children love to use rhythmic movement with "Bydlo" or to accompany it with classroom instruments, particularly sandblocks on the steady eighth notes. Other instruments, of course, may be added as the crescendo develops to its fullest.

"March of the Dwarfs" (Edvard Grieg)—This little tripartite selection not only emphasizes the

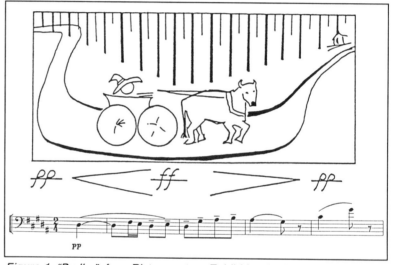

Figure 1. "Bydlo," from Pictures at an Exhibition *by Mussorgsky*

crescendo-decrescendo concept so obvious in "Bydlo" but also emphasizes a midsection that introduces a contrasting mood. The map (figure 2) clearly indicates the ABA form. Both A sections are accompanied by a steady driving bass that alternates hurriedly back and forth between *do* and *sol*, as indicated by the zigzag lines. This gives these two outer sections the character of a fast march. Both also feature a marvelous crescendo and decrescendo. At their peaks, the kettle drum enters loudly, quickly alternating between *do* and *sol* so that these points of arrival are strongly signaled.

I suggest a "Pac-Man" type of rhythmic hand motion to accompany and demonstrate the steadily increasing then decreasing surge of power in these sections. This is done by having the children put

Figure 2. "March of the Dwarfs" by Grieg

Zerlina, flaunting sweet words and his high position to her on the very day she is to be married to a mild-mannered peasant of her own standing. At first, she is hesitant to accept his attention—but gradually, as the music proceeds, she gives in and joins Don Giovanni in a jubilant declaration of love.

The map (figure 3) indicates that the form of the selection is ABA'C. The melodies for each section are given. Also apparent is the fact that Don Giovanni and Zerlina sing in dialogue, rather than together in duet, throughout all of the selection except the final section. Zerlina's hesitancy is strongly suggested at several places by highly chromatic lines that seem to wind and coil

their palms together, and open and shut them like the video-game character's mouth to the steady beat. As the music gets louder and louder, the motions get larger, so that the space between the two hands gets quite wide. The speed is constant.

The slow, peaceful center section, which immediately changes the mode from minor to major, features two solo instruments, the violin and clarinet, as indicated by the map. These play in close succession and are followed by some novel orchestral effects. Children love to sway and bend to the rise and fall of the phrases within this music. Sometimes they will use scarves or streamers to reflect its gentle character. The melodies for sections A and B are presented here.

"La ci darem la mano" from *Don Giovanni* (W. A. Mozart) [2]—This duet ("Here with our hands entwining") presents a musical-dramatic episode wherein the simple country girl Zerlina is enticed and wooed by a suave and sly Don Giovanni. Never missing an opportunity to win over a pretty girl, he shamelessly pursues

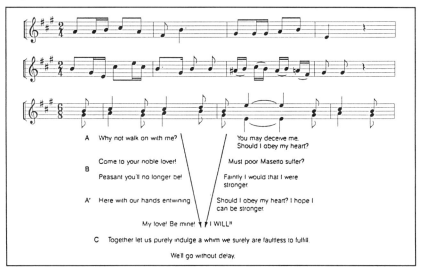

Figure 3. "La ci darem la mano" from Don Giovanni by Mozart

indecisively about a fixed point. Her final consent ("I will!") comes after a downward sequence of three of these vocal gyrations, designating a complete exhaustion and laying aside of resistance. At this point, a buoyant change of meter (from simple duple to compound duple) suggests the joyful bliss and supreme happiness they each feel as they pledge their hearts.

In the upper grades, children like to read the text aloud—the boys taking the lines of Don Giovanni and, in turn, the girls taking the lines of Zerlina. The final three lines are read together. Not only do children find this activity enjoyable, they also find that it gives them insight to Mozart's

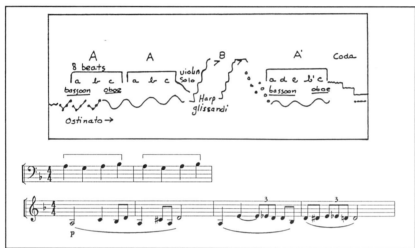

Figure 4. "Berceuse" from The Firebird *by Stravinsky*

superior handling of the text combined with music. Moreover, it seems to bring the whole composition to life through added understanding.

"Berceuse" from ***The Firebird*** (Igor Stravinsky)—According to the ballet story (which comes from an old Russian tale) the Firebird at one point appears and casts a hypnotic spell on a wicked magician who intends to harm the hero, Prince Ivan. This most extraordinary music lulls the villain and his accomplices into a deep, magical sleep.

The selection begins with a tightly knit four-note ostinato that is dreamily reiterated over and over in the harp accompaniment (see figure 4.) Seldom does it change as it underlies all of the A sections. At this point, it is important to recall Stravinsky's masterful use of the ostinato in many other works. Frequently called upon to capture a sense of the status quo, or even stagnation (avoiding musical development according to the Germanic tradition), there is always the sense of rising and falling ten-

sion over their repeated, obstinate statements. This keeps the listener actively engaged. Above this particular ostinato, the languid chromatic melody begins in the bassoon and suggests the Phrygian mode.

The original versions of each of the listening maps presented thus far are in color, and the one in figure 4 is particularly helpful when like sections or phrases are represented with like colors. The overall sectional form AABA' and coda immediately becomes apparent. Particularly interesting are the phrases within the A' section, for here we see that the eight-measure a, b', and c phrases finally return in the bassoon and oboe as we might expect. Stravinsky, however, surprises us and elongates this reprise by inserting two new phrases, d and e. Two ascending glissandi are the dominating features of the central section B. Adding to the exotic flavor and providing a sense of sudden abandon, they also provide brief movement and change from the surrounding music.

Many supplementary classroom activities may accompany the presentation of this wonderful selection. For specific examples, refer to the teacher's manual of *Adventures in Music*.[3] It will be found in most instances, however, that the musical qualities of "Berceuse" are so captivating within their own right that little more than repeated hearings need be emphasized. Children love to point to the appropriate spots of the listening map as the music plays.

Musical Detectives

When used along with their themes, listening maps can be quite important. They can portray moods, dynamics, musical forms, features of the accompaniment, rhythmic organization, instrumentation, and even more. They are fun to create and discuss with the children. During the learning process, children like to think of themselves as musical "detectives," seeking out clues to the music. As aids in helping children internalize and understand music, listening maps encourage a lifelong interest in attentive music listening.

What is learned in one selection can be applied to learning the next. Also, once a specific selection is familiarized and approached through a variety of classroom activities, the listening map can be laid aside. By this point, children will be able to remember and anticipate the features and order of events without help. In other words, they will feel "at home" with the work at hand. This, of course, is ear training or audiation on a high level. At its core is the art of ear analysis, which in large measure should precede visual score analysis. Also at its core is an enjoyment brought forth through understanding.

Notes

1. The listening map for "Berceuse" was created by Jill Guthrie, a graduate student in the author's summer course, 1985. Guthrie teaches at Almeda and Peterson Elementary Schools in the Houston Independent School District.

2. This listening map is based on one created by Roberta Thomason of the Austin Independent School District. It appeared in *Music Contest Bulletin*, published by the University Interscholastic League, Austin, Texas, 1984.

3. *Adventures in Music*, RCA Victor Educational Sales, New York, Grade 2, Vol. 1, p. 27.

Suggested Recordings

Mussorgsky, Modest. "Bydlo." *Adventures in Music*, RCA, Victor Educational Sales, New York, Grade 2, Vol. 1.

Grieg, Edvard. *March of the Dwarfs. Nature and Make Believe.* Bowmar Orchestral Library, Los Angeles, No. 52.

Mozart, Wolfgang Amadeus. "La ci darem la mano." Recordings for *The Enjoyment of Music*, 5th ed., and for *The Norton Scores*, 4th ed. (New York: W. W. Norton and Co.), 1984.

Stravinsky, Igor, "Berceuse," from *The Firebird. Adventures in Music*, RCA Victor Educational Sales, New York. Grade 1, Vol. 1.

MOVEMENT

A very important way for children to become actively involved in music learning is through the use of their natural movement impulses. It is important that music teachers provide extensive movement experiences during the primary years so that children will become comfortable and adept in this important form of expression.

In the articles in this subsection, readers will find ways to include movement while teaching music. Suggestions include both large-group activities—such as singing and moving or learning traditional folk dances—and small-group or individual experiences in improvising movements to music. The authors describe ways of teaching musical concepts incorporating a variety of movement experiences.

Space, Time, & Force: Movement as a Channel to Understanding Music

by Deborah L. Carlson

We all possess body movements with which we express ourselves physically to music. Children use body movements when they play, tumble, fight, or dance, and their natural activity can be an effective vehicle to help them develop an awareness of form, rhythm, tone color, tempo, and dynamics. In *Music with Children*, Grace Nash stated, "Rhythmic experience helps coordination and freedom of expression. Muscular and body coordination enable the individual to move gracefully and confidently. A person will develop a sense of well-being which allows him [or her] to become a more articulate person." [1]

It is essential that these raw materials be organized so that the creator understands what he or she is doing in relation to a particular music concept. Understanding what our body motions are

Deborah L. Carlson is currently Staff Development Coordinator for the Pacific Region (Philippines, Mainland Japan, Okinawa, and Korea) for the U.S. Department of Defense Dependents School, DODDS–Pacific Regional Office, Futenma Box 796, FPO Seattle 98772-0005. This article originally appeared in the September 1980 Music Educators Journal.

capable of doing is the basis of learning how to use movement with music. Leon Karel has written that "our body motions have three aspects. They take place in a given space, they last for a certain amount of time, and they possess a given level of force." [2] To illustrate this point, a person skipping bounces up and down (occupies space), moves quickly (through time), and steps hard while lightly bouncing (exerts force). The three elements of space, time, and force are also indicators of how we feel. For instance, when a person is happy, he or she may walk with long strides, swinging the arms briskly with an enthusiastic spirit.

Rarely, though, are the three elements of movement separate entities; combinations of space, time, and force are typically used. Figure 1 illustrates how certain movements relate to these elements. In order for movement to be expressive, it is necessary to use space, time, and force as an integration of unity and variety, contrast and climax, and repetition. These "parts" of the whole closely parallel components of music. Using music with an ABA form, for example, the same movement combination used in the beginning of a work could be repeated at its conclusion. Understanding the elements of movement and how they can be put together is essential before attempting to teach music through movement.

Look for children who seem to move awkwardly, and make an effort to gear part of the movement session so that they can feel involved without being

Movement	Space	Time	Force
Spiral	Up or down	Fast or slow	Smooth, continuous
Slide	Side to side	Moderately fast	Tension-release
Turn	Curved	Slow, steady	Forceful
Push	Straight line	Fast	Percussive, quick short

Figure 1.

Movement Activities, K–4

Children in kindergarten through the fourth grade are interested in exploring what their bodies can do, and they have not had much experience with the context or technical aspects of music or movement. Giving the students a firm foundation in the basics of music and movement when they are unafraid to express themselves will free them, as they grow older, to be more creative in matching movements to concepts in music.

From the beginning, children need to "think about the behavior before doing it," as Bryant Cratty suggests.[3] Using "Singing in the Seven Way," from the song collection by C. Clark Bell *Mixed Meters for Minors* (see figure 2) as an example of metric accents (1–2, 1–2, 1–2–3), ask the children to think of movements that reflect the rhythms.[4] You could begin by asking, "If I turn, and turn, and keep turning, will I be feeling the meter?" Do this to show the children it would not be effective. After listening to their ideas, suggest a way; for example, try clap-patschen-clap-patschen-clap-clap-clap, or step-slide-step-slide-step-step-step. Encourage them to think through the movement and then execute it. Most likely, after they have been asked to listen to the music, create their own movement, think about how the teacher would demonstrate it, perform it, and then create a different movement to it, the children will be able to recognize and feel the meter in still other songs.

embarrassed. "The Circle Song"[5] (see Figure 3) is in 12/8 time and encourages the use of the imagination while keeping up with the meter. It begins with walking around the circle "one by one," and everybody can be involved in the first part of this song. There is not enough time for each person to walk around the circle, stepping or clapping out the meter, while pretending he or she is some kind of animal, an ice cream cone, or whatever. However, the whole class can join hands and walk around in a circle to step out the meter. The next part of the song has the students walking "two by two" and then "three by three." Here, there is room for individualizing. The whole class can become involved now; those who want to participate in pairs of two and groups of three may branch out and be imaginative, while the rest of the class remains in the circle keeping time with various nonlocomotor movements. Can the children keep time to the music with their body movements? After three verses, each child will have had the opportunity to use nonlocomotor movement in the circle in illustrating 12/8 meter and an opportunity to skip around the circle with locomotor movement in time with the singing.

Rhythmic folk songs from various cultures (for example, the Israeli song "Zum Gali Gali") can be used effectively to teach the skill of listening before moving. The students must be familiar with such songs before they can know

Figure 2. "Singing in the Seven Way," from Mixed Meters for Minors. *Words and music by C. Clark Bell. It may help to practice L-R-R-L-R-L-R patschen and then reverse to do L-R-L-R-L-R-R. You may also "sweeten" up the chords by adding sevenths, ninths, elevenths, and thirteenths.*

when to move. In listening, they should pay especially close attention to the interplay of verses and refrains.

When the children have begun to feel meter, recognize form, and work together on creative movement, they can attempt to act out a story-song by using motions to create images. A good selection for this purpose is "Grandpa Builds a Table."[6] Grandpa's tools can be used as devices to teach children the concept of force. For example, when they are asked to use movement to depict a buzz saw, how much energy goes into it? How hard must you pound when using a hammer? How fluid should the swish of a paintbrush be? By working with the child on the use of different energy levels connected to familiar items, such as tools, the teacher lays the groundwork for the students to transfer this learning to understanding similar concepts in other types of music. After each of Grandpa's tools has been introduced in this song, a measure of instrumental music follows during which the students may prepare to illustrate the next tool.

Tempo and dynamics are vital to musical expression. To begin to help children become sensitive to tempo, introduce a simple, rhythmic march such as "The

Fast and Slow March." [7] The work begins fast, slows down, and then speeds up again; and the clipped percussive background adds an air of excitement to the students' movements. The children must listen carefully in order to respond appropriately to the tempo changes. The volume does not change when the tempo does, but there will be a tendency to "tiptoe quietly" and "stamp loudly" when the march changes tempo. The Japanese folk tune "Teru Teru Bozu" [8] uses several types of drums, chimes, and sounds not commonly heard in American music. It is a composition with varying dynamics and definite possibilities for expressive movements. There are up-and-down feelings with the chimes, strong rhythmic beats on the drum, and a soft, flowing melody—all providing an opportunity for the children to use their creativity in responding to dynamics and mood.

Although successful experiences encourage other movement activities, children in the primary grades need some direction to minimize confusion or frustration. Providing an opportu-

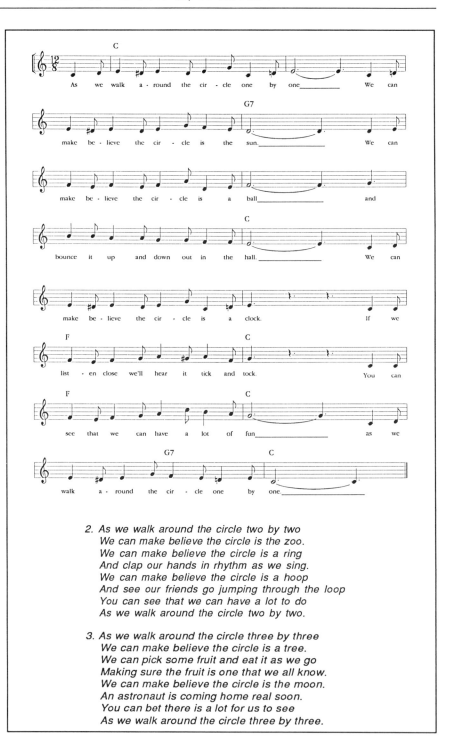

2. As we walk around the circle two by two
   We can make believe the circle is the zoo.
   We can make believe the circle is a ring
   And clap our hands in rhythm as we sing.
   We can make believe the circle is a hoop
   And see our friends go jumping through the loop
   You can see that we can have a lot to do
   As we walk around the circle two by two.

3. As we walk around the circle three by three
   We can make believe the circle is a tree.
   We can pick some fruit and eat it as we go
   Making sure the fruit is one that we all know.
   We can make believe the circle is the moon.
   An astronaut is coming home real soon.
   You can bet there is a lot for us to see
   As we walk around the circle three by three.

Figure 3. "The Circle Song," from Mixed Meters for Minors. *Words and music by C. Clark Bell. Try writing another verse about "four by four." This song may feel like there are four beats per measure; therefore, try feeling that each beat has three parts. Copyright ©1975 by Clark Bell, PO Box 1237, Boca Raton, FL 33432. International copyright secured. Printed in the USA. All rights reserved.*

nity for children to feel accomplished reinforces their self-confidence and builds a foundation for creative, independent self-expression.

Suggestions for Middle School Students

Fifth- through eighth-grade students understand music concepts in a more sophisticated manner because they build on the experiences they had in the primary grades. For example, more instrumental works can be used rather than songs telling the students what to do. By now, the students should have developed some sense of independence and should not feel so self-conscious about moving. The authors of *Interpreting Music Through Movement* assert that "Bach, Beethoven, and Brahms are not necessarily first aims for all children. Good modern popular music, charming in melody and strong in rhythmic power, provides some of the finest tools available for freeing children from inhibitions and making them want to respond with expressive movement." [9]

The instrumental composition "Baroque and Blue" [10] for flute and piano includes several contrasting movements in which the meter changes back and forth from triple to duple time. The students might use locomotion to represent the triplets and nonlocomotion to feel the duple meter. One way to express levels of energy and force is to step strongly on the first beat of the triplet and to rise up on the toes for the second and third pulses. When the mood changes, the students might change from heavy nonlocomotor arm movements to twirling locomotor ones. It is not necessary for everyone to move in the same way, but each student should be able to recognize when the change occurs and respond appropriately.

In Isao Tomita's "Baba Yaga," [11] electronic instruments create sounds that resemble types of movement, such as a spiral, a whirl, or hard stamping. This work is conducive to throwing the complete body into exhaustive movement and then, suddenly, into a creeping, eerie crawl. The difference in sounds produced in "Baba Yaga" compared to those found in a more standard composition encourages creative movement, but the levels of intensity vary so radically that the students must

be in complete control in order to quickly switch movements.

Jimmy Webb's "MacArthur Park" as performed by Maynard Ferguson [12] provides students with a lesson on repetition. The first four measures are repeated in different keys by various groups of instruments. When used as a listening exercise prior to movement, the students can figure out how many times the four measures are played, and then verbally describe how the theme varies each time. Or, the class can be divided into four groups: The first group is assigned the task of developing a pattern of locomotion for the first four repetitions of the theme; the second group can use nonlocomotion for the next four repetitions; the third group uses only their arms to express changes in dynamics of the last four repetitions; and the last group uses their legs in locomotion to emphasize the tempo of all the repetitions of the theme.

Movement is a form of self-expression that capitalizes on the same concepts used in music—time, space, and force. It is a natural part of children's activities, both before formal education begins and afterward. If movement is integral to the music program, the students will have a means of relating new concepts in music to the familiar sense of rhythmic security and independence inherent in their bodies.

Notes

With the exception of the material by C. Clark Bell, which is currently available, the songs and other resources suggested in this article may be difficult to obtain; however, the author's ideas are easily adapted to newer publications.—ED.

1. Grace C. Nash, *Music with Children* (Kitching Educational Division of Ludwig Industries, 1970).

2. Leon C. Karel, *Avenues to the Arts* (Kirksville, MO: Simpson Publishing Company, 1969).

3. Bryant J. Cratty, *Some Educational Implications of Movements* (Seattle: Special Child Publications, 1971).

4. "Singing in the Seven Way," *Mixed Meters for Minors* (Boca Raton, FL: Clark Bell Productions, 1975).

5. "The Circle Song," *Mixed Meters for Minors* (Boca Raton, FL: Clark Bell Productions, 1975).

6. "Grandpa Builds a Table," *Creative Movement and Rhythmic Express* (Hap Palmer, Educational Activities, Inc., 1969).

7. "Fast and Slow March," *Creative Movement and Rhythmic Expression* (Hap Palmer, Educational Activities, Inc., 1969).

8. "Teru Teru Bozu," *Rhythms Today!* (Morristown, NJ: Silver Burdett Company, 1965).

9. Louise Humphreys and Jerrold Ross, *Interpreting Music Through Movement* (Englewood Cliffs, NJ: Prentice-Hall, Inc., 1964).

10. "Baroque and Blue," *Suite for Flute and Jazz Piano* (Columbia, 33233).

11. "Baba Yaga," *Pictures at an Exhibition* (RCA, ARL 1-0838).

12. "MacArthur Park," *M. F. Horn* (Columbia, C-30466).

Selected Readings

Bell, C. Clark. *Mixed Meters for Minors.* Clark Bell Productions, PO Box 1237, Boca Raton, FL 33432.

Cratty, Bryant J. *Some Educational Implications of Movements.* Seattle: Special Child Publications, 1971.

Dalcroze, Emile Jaques. *Rhythm, Music and Education.* Great Britain: The Dalcroze Society, Inc. 1973.

Findlay, Elsa, *Rhythm and Movement: Applications of Dalcroze Eurhythmics.* Evanston, IL: Summy-Birchard Company, 1971.

Humphreys, Louise and Jerrold Ross, *Interpreting Music Through Movement.* Englewood Cliffs, NJ: Prentice-Hall, Inc. 1964.

Karel, Leon C. *Avenues to the Arts.* Kirksville, MO: Simpson Publishing Company, 1969.

Nash, Grace C. *Music With Children.* Kitching Educational Division of Ludwig Industries, 1970.

Sheehy, Emma D. *Children Discover Music and Dance.* New York: Teachers College Press, Columbia University, 1968.

Selected Recordings

"Baroque and Blue," *Suite for Flute and Jazz Piano* (Columbia, 33233).

Best of Mixed Meters for Minors. Audiocassette or CD (Clark Bell Productions, PO Box 1237, Boca Raton, FL 33432).

"The Circle Song," *Mixed Meters for Minors* (Clark Bell Productions, PO Box 1237, Boca Raton, FL 33432).

"Fast and Slow March," *Creative Movement and Rhythmic Expression* (Hap Palmer, Educational Activities, Inc., AR533).

Ferguson, Maynard, "MacArthur Park," *M. F. Horn* (Columbia, C-30466).

"Grandpa Builds a Table," *Creative Movement and Rhythmic Expression* (Hap Palmer, Educational Activities, Inc., AR533).

"Singing in the Seven Way," *Mixed Meters for Minors* (Clark Bell Productions, PO Box 1237, Boca Raton, FL 33432).

"Teru Teru Bozu," *Rhythms Today!* (Silver Burdett Company, 8118POO).

Tomita, Isao, "Baba Yaga," *Pictures at an Exhibition* (RCA, ARL1-0838).

Elementary Music Con Moto

by Jack Neill

L et's face it: children love to move. They thrive on walking, running, jumping, fidgeting, bouncing, hopping, gesturing, skipping, mimicking, racing, and dancing. Typically, the elementary student is in motion all of his or her waking hours; a truly child-centered teaching approach must attempt to develop skills, concepts, and aesthetics in students by drawing on this constant impulse for movement. Although this is not impossible, it is not always easy to do with subjects like reading, math, and spelling. The elementary music teacher, however, is in the enviable position of readily being able to direct this natural energy toward real learning.

From the moment of birth, a child's development is measured in movement skills. The ability to hold the head erect, to turn over, to sit up, to coordinate the hands and eyes, to crawl, to stand, to walk, to skip, and to gallop are all memorable events and milestones in a child's growth. Indeed, most schools today recognize that children who have difficulty in acquiring basic movement skills require special attention.

The inseparable connection between music and movement has been demonstrated to be an effective means to musical development by many educa-

Jack Neill is a music specialist in the Manassas, Virginia, Public Schools; he currently teaches at Baldwin Elementary School. This article originally appeared in the January 1990 Music Educators Journal.

tors, most notably Emile Jaques-Dalcroze and Carl Orff. This bond is most obvious in dance music, where the rhythms, meter, tempo, style, and form of the music are a response to the body's movement in performing the dance. There are other striking examples, however: The rhythms and meter of the mother's lullaby are directly drawn from the motion of rocking the baby to sleep, and the meter and style of sea shanties are derived from the movements of the laborers aboard ship. Innumerable traditional children's songs include rhythms that reflect motions of the games being played during their singing. The marriage of music and movement is demonstrated every time a young child marches exuberantly to the beat of a band during a parade or spontaneously invents dance movements to a song on the radio. Because of this close relationship, musical elements such as rhythm, meter, style, form, tempo, and dynamics can be conceptually explored and developed through movement.

How often do we concentrate on the visual and aural learners in our classes while neglecting those students who learn best in the tactile and kinesthetic modes? These are the students who actually need to touch and to experience physically what they are being taught before learning can begin. There are probably more of these children in your classes than you might expect.

Movement for Teachers

Teachers who shy away from using body movement as a teaching technique express several reasons for doing so. Many simply don't feel comfortable with movement. Undoubtedly, much of this discomfort stems from the fact that most of us were trained as instrumentalists or as vocalists. In either case, our music teachers frowned on extraneous movement. How often did we hear, "Sit still on that bench while you play," or "Can't you sing that without tapping your foot or swaying like that?" If we have the best interest of our students at heart, we will overcome this shortcoming in our own educations. Start slowly. Try some simple activities in private, and do not be upset if you feel somewhat awkward at first. Bear with it, and remember the words of George Bernard Shaw, who said that you cannot learn to skate without looking ridiculous—the ice of life is slippery. A surprising measure of comfort and confidence will quickly be attained.

Some teachers use the excuse of inadequate space and facilities to attempt to justify their neglect of movement education. Resourceful teachers can solve this problem by moving desks and chairs to one side of the room, using hallways and lobbies, going outdoors in good weather, or arranging an occasional "room swap" with the gym teacher. Others fear that movement activities will encourage inappropriate behavior and lead to an increase in discipline problems. Control can be maintained quite easily if a few simple "ground rules" are enforced: (1) No one may touch any person or thing unless told to do so; (2) No one may move "out of bounds" (that is, into any part of the room that is beyond the limits determined at the beginning of class by the teacher); (3) When the signal is given to stop, everyone must stop—properly balanced on two feet.

There are some people who hold the mistaken belief that physical education classes adequately provide for students' needs in movement. They obviously have not taken into account the fact that sedentary leisure-time activities such as television viewing and video-game playing have robbed children of some of the prime opportunities for developing movement skills and rhythmic coordination. Also, although the avid soccer player and gymnast may have acquired considerable skill, even these students need a teacher's guidance to relate these

skills to musical learning and to discover the inherent aesthetic possibilities in movement.

First Steps

The first step in assisting students—and teachers—to feel comfortable with movement is to approach it with a positive attitude; do not be apologetic or tentative when beginning movement activities. Let the students know that you expect them to succeed and to learn. Begin by exploring some nonlocomotor movements: bending, straightening, twisting, swinging, swaying, pushing, pulling, shaking, spreading, and other activities that do not require movement away from the starting space. Initially, students will probably perform these movements using only their arms; you must encourage them to try other parts of their bodies as well: "Find a different part of your body to shake." "Twist two different parts at once." "Bend one part of your body at the same time you straighten another part." Encourage them to vary direction (upward, downward, forward, backward, sideward, inward, outward) and level (high, low, medium) as well.

Have students, working together as pairs, create a rondo—ABACADAEA—of nonlocomotor movements. Make one student responsible for sections B and D, the other for sections C and E, and make them both responsible for the A sections. Share these "mini-choreographies" with the class. Mirror games, in which one student imitates or mirrors the activities of another, offer additional opportunities to explore nonlocomotor movements.

Locomotor movements are motions that require more space (such as walking, running, jumping, hopping, skipping, galloping, sliding, and bouncing). Once again, insist that students vary the direction, level, and speed of their movements. Often students who feel self-conscious during the activities will be more comfortable if they can "impersonate" other people or machines: Ask them to walk like a robot, like a monster, like they are walking on ice, like they are walking on hot sand, or as if they are wearing lead shoes. Instruct them to run like a jogger, like they are in slow motion, like they are running through deep water, or like they are running uphill. Students can move with a partner, trying such exercises as jumping together with one finger touching one of a partner's fingers, without letting their fingers separate; skipping together with one elbow touching the partner's elbow; or walking together with their backs touching.

Accompaniments and Images

Accompany the students' locomotor movements instrumentally. Direct their listening to the accompaniment and ask them to react to it: "Stop whenever you hear a key change." "Change partners every time the meter changes." "Let your movements reflect the tempo changes." "Jump whenever you hear a syncopated rhythm."

Combine locomotor and nonlocomotor movement in a "generic circle dance." Use music with an easily definable beat, in duple meter and with regular phrasing. Have the students imitate your motions (or those of another leader), alternating locomotor and nonlocomotor movement. For example, ask them to alternate sixteen beats of walking, sixteen beats of hopping, and sixteen beats of swaying. The class may wish to organize these movements into a structured sequence. Students might devise a logical method to notate their choreography so that it can be learned by another class.

Another classic technique for developing students' confidence in movement skills is to use machine images. Individual students can perform movements that characterize household machines—such as toasters or washing machines. Similarly, several students can be parts of one giant contraption in which the machinelike movements of each student relate to and complement the others. Another group can accompany the movement with appropriate vocal sounds or classroom percussion instruments. If the movements are performed at several different speeds, this accompaniment can be the start of an exploration of polymeter.

Simple folk dances offer even more possibilities for a teacher with limited experience to present meaningful and satisfying movement activities to students. Recordings with easy-to-follow instructions can be found in many record stores and catalogs. Try a few at first and, once you and your students have mastered them, gradually increase your repertoire.

Form and Style

Try moving in canon: you should improvise a movement that is imitated by the class at a specified time interval (initially, after four or eight beats). After the class gains confidence, try movement canons in four or more parts. Movement sequences can easily be invented to reflect simple musical forms such as ABA or rondo. The concepts of theme and variations can also be expressed in movement. The teacher makes a very simple motion; the students in turn create variants of the original motion.

Use recorded music of all styles. Students can step the pulse while clapping the first beat of each measure, or vice-versa. They can walk to a recurring rhythmic pattern while clapping the hand of someone they happen to pass on the first beat of a new phrase. There is no end to the possibilities. Don't forget to investigate students' ball games, jump-rope games, and playground chants that involve body movement. How can you aim these toward musical growth? Have you ever tried to bounce a ball steadily in 2/4, 6/8, or 7/8 meter? How about trying to bounce a ball to a sequence of two measures of each of these meters?

Once you and your students have begun moving in the music classroom, you will probably be on the lookout for new ideas. The books listed in the "Suggested Readings" for this article are among many excellent ones that provide additional practical suggestions that will help keep your classes in motion.

If we are indeed serious about conceptual learning, skills development, and aesthetic education, we cannot afford to neglect one of the most basic impulses children possess—the need to move. In the words of the renowned musicologist, Curt Sachs:

> The dance is the mother of the arts. Music and poetry exist in time; painting and architecture in space. But the dance lives at once in time and space. The creator and the thing created, the artist and the work are still one and the same

thing. Rhythmical patterns of movement, the plastic sense of space, the vivid representation of a world seen and imagined—these things man creates in his own body in the dance before he uses substance and stone and word to give expression to his inner experiences.[1]

Note

1. Curt Sachs, *World History of the Dance*, translated by Bessie Schonberg (New York: Norton, 1963), 3.

Suggested Readings

Boorman, Joyce, *Dance and Language Experiences With Children*. Ontario, Canada: Longman, 1973.

Fleming, Gladys A. *Creative Rhythmic Movement*. Englewood Cliffs, NJ: Prentice-Hall, 1976.

Haselbach, Barbara. *Dance Education*. Translated by Margaret Murray. London: Schott, 1978.

Murray, Ruth Lowell. *Dance in Elementary Education*. New York: Harper & Row, 1975.

Nelson, Esther L. *Dancing Games for Children of All Ages*. New York: Sterling, 1973.

_____. *Movement Games for Children of All Ages*. New York: Sterling, 1973.

Weikart, Phyllis S. *Movement Plus Rhymes, Songs, and Singing Games*. Ypsilanti, MI: High/Scope, 1988

_____. *Teaching Movement and Dance*. Ypsilanti, MI: High/Scope, 1982.

Teaching Music Through Balkan Folk Dance

by Patricia Shehan Campbell

Folk dancing in school settings has long been within the domain of the physical education instructor. At the elementary and middle school levels, circle, square, and partner dances are used to develop motor coordination, laterality, directionality, and spatial orientation skills. Educators justify the inclusion of folk dance in the curriculum for the development of such social skills as group cooperation and interaction, for the reinforcement of positive attitudes toward school and education, for the provision of added enrichment to the school program, and for exposure to the folkways of various world regions.

Coordinated movements of the body are a means of physical expression, and the recreational uses of folk dance are a preferred activity for people of all ages. The urge to coordinate movements of the body in response to an internal or external rhythm is a characteristic of the human organism that knows no cultural bounds. Movement becomes an art form when isolated gestures and actions are organized into deliberate patterns. Like music, forms of the dance adhere to the universal principles of tension and release, a forward progression toward

Patricia Shehan Campbell is an associate professor of music education at the University of Washington, Seattle. This article originally appeared in the November 1984 Music Educators Journal.

a cadence, a sense of unity through the repetition of gestures and step patterns, and variety through contrasting patterns.

Movement Education in Music

Scientific research in neurophysiology has suggested a close relationship between motor activity and mental activity, such that movement may facilitate and enhance conceptual learning. In music, as in all learning, the mind and body function as a totality, and the sensory feedback from movement is related to higher mental processes. Learning is thought to be a three-part process that activates the neuromuscular system: (1) music as a sensory stimulus generates a natural motor response, (2) the movement experience sets up a mental image or concept of a rhythm, melody, or formal musical design, and (3) through the use of symbols such as words or notation, intellectualization occurs.

Some techniques in music education—including Dalcroze, Orff, and Kodály—use movement as an essential part of the learning process. The eurhythmics approach of Emile Jaques-Dalcroze is a training method in musical rhythm through body experience. Based on the idea that the source of music rhythms is the locomotor rhythms of the body, the student is trained to react quickly to music by seeing, hearing, feeling, and thinking it at the same time. As opposed to ballet and modern dance, which stress communicating through movement, the Dalcroze objective is to allow the individual to feel music through a total physical experience.

The Orff approach views music, movement, and speech as inseparable and fundamental to the music education of children. Untrained natural actions are encouraged, related to music, and used in shaping musical concepts. Spontaneous play activities that incorporate movement are the basis for the development of a rhythmic sense, and clapping, stamping, snapping, and patting are critical behaviors for knowing musical rhythms and forms.

The Kodály system of music education shares with Orff the belief that movement is natural for children. Traditional folk dances are used as part of the sequence of music learning in Hungary, where children learn basic pulse and rhythmic patterns through movement. Another distinctive feature of the Kodály technique is the use of hand signs associated with pitches, gestures that give a visual and kinetic perspective to melody.

The potential of folk dance has largely been neglected by music specialists as a means for teaching rhythm and meter, despite its simplicity as a progression of easy foot patterns that combine elements of time and space. The adage is true that "if you can walk, you can folk dance," and there is a varied and extensive repertory of dances to accommodate even the beginner. Folk dance can be successfully used in the elementary school, where children are less resistant to movement activities, and there is a certain natural and spontaneous storehouse of rhythmic behaviors in this early stage of development. Secondary school experiences in folk dance can be rewarding when the instruction is enthusiastic and well paced.

Duple and triple meters, and even complex irregular meters, can become clear through folk dance. The odd, uneven, or composite meters that surface in the works of Igor Stravinsky and Béla Bartók are found also in the music of southeastern European folk dances. Through physical involvement in the footwork of the dance, students and teachers can confront the intellectual and psychomotor problems associated with contemporary meters and rhythms.

Balkan Dance in America

It is imperative that school music programs feature a variety of styles for a more global perspective on the nature of music. For example, the rhythmically sophisticated music of the Balkan region of southeastern Europe accompanies one of the richest collections of folk dances in the world. The Balkans encompass the nations of [the former] Yugoslavia (Macedonia, Montenegro, Bosnia-Herzogovina, Serbia, Croatia, and Slovenia), Bulgaria, Albania, Romania, and Greece. This area stands at a crossroads between the European and Asian worlds, so that cross-fertilization from both East and West has occurred quite naturally.

Balkan people have been coming to the New World since Colonial times, but they did not arrive in numbers sufficient to establish permanent communities until the 1890s. In the first three decades of this century, Europeans from eastern and southern Europe far outnumbered those arriving from western and northern Europe. Today, the U.S. population consists of 3 percent southeastern European immigrants or their descendants, with substantial communities in such midwestern cities as Chicago, Detroit, Cleveland, Pittsburgh, and St. Louis. Their churches are important social centers where ethnic awareness, language, and traditions are maintained. Nearly every community supports dance, choral, and instrumental ensembles. Music is a link to the past that preserves and popularizes Balkan traditions.

The traditional music of the Balkan folk dance can best be described through the six characteristics of music (melody, rhythm, texture, timbre, dynamics, and form). Although there are common threads found in all European folk music, such as strophic form and metric rhythms linked closely to poetry, the music of southeastern Europe is distinguished by a strong Islamic influence. The Middle Eastern flavor becomes most apparent in the sometimes nasalized vocal quality, the heterophonic texture in which performers sound simultaneous variations of the main melody, and the irregular metric groupings. Instruments such as the Greek double-reed "zornah" and Bulgarian bagpipes called "gaida" (which have a melody pipe and, unlike the highland pipes of Scotland, only one drone pipe) originated in the Middle East. They were brought to the region by the Turks during their five-hundred-year occupation.

Learning Sequence

In a musical approach to folk dance, a sequence of steps that combines listening and motor skills may best reinforce the rhythmic aspects of the music. Assuming that students can identify a steady pulse in a musical selection, and that the movement environment is nonthreatening, the following folk dance teaching/learning sequence is suggested:

1. As introduction to the musical style of the dance accompaniment, it is essential to listen to the music in a guided way that directs students' attention to the discovery of the instruments, recurring rhythmic patterns, melodic range and motifs, repeated and contrasting sections, and chordal, unison, or heterophonic textures. Individual listening tasks can be assigned to small groups to give greater focus, or several listenings can be planned with a specific class assignment each time. The familiarity that develops through repeated listenings is likely to create a more comfortable dance experience, and the music may also become better understood and appreciated.

2. Students should then be directed to listen and respond to the underlying rhythm sounded in the bass line or chordal accompaniment. By patting or clapping these accented beats, students are putting the eventual footwork into their hands. The physical realization of the rhythmic framework is a major breakthrough in learning the dance.

3. Students use descriptive words to indicate the motion of the dance. By chanting words like "walk," "lift," and "touch" to the patted rhythms, they will more easily perform the necessary movements of the feet.

4. The transfer of movement from the hands to the feet then occurs. The repeated rhythm chant should continue, so that students match the footwork to the descriptive words. This speech-action activity may be more successful without the music, which may confuse those individuals who attend to

other musical aspects such as timbre and melodic rhythm.

5. In the final stage, the music returns to accompany the movement. Students are instructed to internalize the rhythm chant, thinking the descriptive words while dancing. The rhythm should so totally become a part of the mind-body connection that students return full circle to the music, the essential component of the experience.

The proposed progression is fundamental for learning the music as well as the dance. It is flexible enough to allow for differences in age, motor skills, and experience. Younger children or those with handicapping conditions will require more time at each stage. The music-language-movement-music sequence is most effective when experienced in that order. Middle school students or those with considerable previous movement experience are likely to advance quickly through the process. If slower tempos are taken at first, chants and movement should be restored to the actual speed before advancing to the next stage.

Four Balkan Dances

Figure 1 shows a folk song from a Yugoslavian dance that features 7/8 meter. A loose English translation is provided. Note the division of the melodic rhythm into 3-2-2, which is heard as two uneven groups of 3 and 4 in the underlying rhythmic accompaniment. The dance pattern is structured to include two uneven steps per measure, and is completed and repeated at the end of three measures throughout the entire song.

Figure 2 gives the dance rhythms to four important Balkan folk dances. The steps are correlated with the rhythmic pattern, and these descriptive words are spoken to the indicated rhythm. In all cases, the dance begins with the weight on the left foot, so that the right foot begins the pattern to the right direction. Walking steps are designated as "walk"; a "lift" is a movement of the foot off the floor with the knee slightly bent; and to "step" is to touch the foot to the floor without giving full weight. Note that leaps, hops, skips, and jumps are avoided in these beginning dances. The addition of a light bounce to these basic steps captures the spirit of the dance; the music is the guide to this finishing touch. If the recommended recordings are not available, others can be substituted quite readily, as the dances featured are among the most common.

The song "Macedonian Girl" accompanies the *lesnoto,* a very popular village dance of southern Yugoslavia. The steps are basic and demand little concentrated effort once they are learned, so that conversation flows as the people dance. The formation is in a line, with a handhold that appears as a "W" between two dancers, the elbows bent.

Tsamiko (sam-ee-ko) was originally danced by Greek warriors who staged battles against the Turks in the northern mountains during the Greek War of Independence. Today, the line dance is still led by men who wheel and leap, turning midair somersaults as a show of physical skill and agility.

Serbians and Croatians have danced the *kolo* for centuries, often in close circles with the arms at the sides in an inverted "V" handhold. The important tambouritza ensemble consisting of various sizes of pear-shaped plucked lutes plays a lively accompaniment to the duple-metered dance. An array of complex

Figure 1. "Macedonian Girl" (Makedonsko Devojce), recorded on World Tone 10001

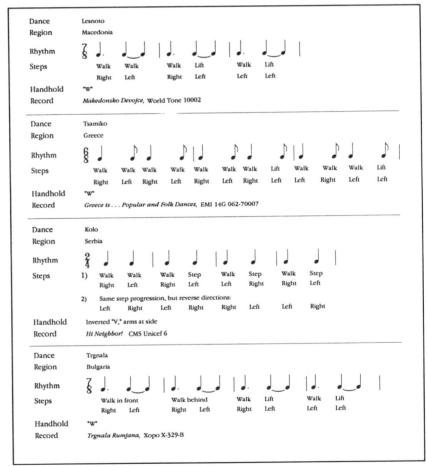

Figure 2. Dance rhythms and step patterns

variations on the basic step pattern challenges the more experienced dancers.

An easy dance is the *trgnala* (trig-nah-lah), which combines steps and lifts with the "grapevine" technique of crossing in front and behind the weighted stationery foot. Like the lesnoto, this easy dance is performed in a line formation using the "W" handhold. Although the music directs the beginner to move in irregular rhythm to the alternating groups of three and four pulses per measure, students can choose to syncopate their movement to the music by stepping evenly every 3½ beats.

In addition to the by-products of intercultural understanding and sense of community spirit that result from folk dance, an understanding of southeastern European traditional music can be reinforced through the experiential approach. Specialists who stress the musical merits of Balkan dance may then effectively transfer the concepts to other musical styles. For the music educator, the emphasis in folk dance is on the mind-body connection that enhances music learning.

Discography

General

Hi Neighbor! CMS Unicef, 1–18. Includes songs and dances from Greece and Yugoslavia.

The Whole World Sings, Electra EKS 206. Dance songs from Greece, Romania, Israel, Russia.

Folk Instruments of the World, Follet L24. Instrumental selections from Bulgaria, Hungary, Russia, Serbia, Greece, and other world regions.

The Nonesuch Explorer, Nonesuch H/11. Includes songs from Bulgaria, Greece, and Yugoslavia.

Bulgaria

Folk Music of Bulgaria, Topic 12 T 107.

A Harvest, a Shepherd, a Bride: Village Music of Bulgaria, Nonesuch H-72034.

In the Shadow of the Mountain: Bulgarian Folk Music, Nonesuch H-72038.

Greece

Bouzouki: The Music of Greece, Nonesuch H-72004.

Greece Is . . . Popular and Folk Dances, EMI 14G 062-70007.

Greece Is . . . Dances, EMI 14G 062-70008.

Greek Folk Dances, Monitor MFS 417.

Yugoslavia

Folk Music of Yugoslavia, Ethnic Folkways FE 4434.

Macedonia Songs and Dances, Monitor MFS 736.

Songs and Dances of Macedonia, Request SRLP 8136.

Village Music of Yugoslavia, Nonesuch H-72042.

CREATING

All children need to have experiences not only in recreating the music of others, but also in creating their own forms of musical expression. Opportunities to develop simple or elaborate music are based, of course, on preliminary experiences with musical concepts. Musical creativity can begin with sound exploration using body and vocal sounds in addition to traditional classroom instruments, or teachers can provide creative experiences using improvisatory opportunities such as those espoused by the Orff Schulwerk approach. Musical creation can also occur in the writing of class songs, through small-group composition projects, and via individual compositions. In all of these varied active encounters with musical materials, children experience the process of composition and become more deeply involved in music learning.

Whispers, Growls, Screams, and Puffs . . . Lead to Composition

by Malcolm J. Tait

Can children compose their own music in the classroom in the way they paint their own pictures, write their own stories or poems, and make up their own dances? The possibilities for this kind of creative activity in music can be explored through four interrelated phases. The first phase emphasizes sound exploration and discovery; the second associates sounds with a wide range of imagery; the third analyzes and groups sounds in terms of their inherent characteristics; and the fourth records and preserves the sounds, if this is deemed desirable.

Discovering Sounds

Sound exploration and discovery involves both the voice and instruments. Children can explore their own voices with closed-mouth and open-mouth sounds. They can produce sounds of indefinite pitch such as whispers, growls, screams, and puffs,

Malcom J. Tait is dean of the School of Music at East Carolina University, Greenville, North Carolina. This article originally appeared in the February 1971 Music Educators Journal.

or they can create more precise pitch levels by humming, whistling, and chanting. Surfaces and objects such as walls and desks, as well as containers of every shape and size, are capable of producing a wide variety of sounds. Hitting, scraping, tapping, plucking, and a host of other techniques can all lead to interesting sound discoveries. Classroom and orchestra instruments are perhaps most frequently experienced in a context of skill development, but they can also be explored in terms of their sound potential for children's compositions.

Associating Sounds with Imagery

Obviously, in order to approach musical composition, children need to move beyond this exploratory and discovery phase. Although it can be a pleasant enough experience to explore a wide variety of sounds, the process needs some structuring before it can represent musical composition. This is where imagery can play a legitimate role insofar as it associates sounds with ideas, feelings, colors, or shapes. By working with groups of sounds based on associated imagery, children can identify and produce sounds that evoke a range of feelings such as happiness, anger, excitement, or sadness. They can create sounds that suggest qualities of movement such as stretching, relaxing, or bouncing. The sounds we associate with nature—rain, thunder, wind, sea, and animals—offer further possible groupings. There are also mechanically produced sounds such as those found in the street, the kitchen, or the factory. Sometimes we associate shapes, colors, and textures with sounds. Finally, there are the more obvious verbal sound associations involving simple stories, nursery rhymes, and poems or plays.

A teacher can direct students to "Play the drum to help us stretch. Find some sounds to make us afraid. Make your voice sound like the sea. Create some sounds that would go with this picture." For more extended compositions, children can build diaries of sound events associated with building sites, space trips, storms, and so on. A large-group activity may produce a sound mural in which each child works independently while contributing to a larger tonal image. In each instance, the associated idea or image provides a framework for the music just as a libretto provides a framework for the music in an opera.

Understanding Music's Components

The third phase of classroom composition focuses on the fundamental characteristics of sounds—length, loudness, pitch, and quality. I am not suggesting that sound imagery should cease when this phase begins; after all, our greatest composers used quite specific imagery in operas and oratorios as well as in instrumental and orchestra compositions.

Children should become more aware of sound elements so that they can use them to say what they want to say with more precision. This is a period when children begin to strengthen sound discovery and imagery with knowledge of the media. To do this, they need to respond and work with the inner components of sounds.

Whereas such concepts as pulse, tempo, pitch, dynamics, and accent have been implicit in earlier phases of discovery and imagery, they now become explicit and take on personal meanings. They are now viewed in the context of sound phenomena,

as well as in terms of their expressive potential. Similarly, concepts such as introduction, repetition, imitation, and variation provide a means of extending compositions and of binding them into cohesive shapes.

During this phase, a teacher encourages children to "Sing an answer to this question. Extend this phrase. Vary this pattern. Imitate this motif. Change the dynamics. Increase the tempo. Vary the accent." More innovative teachers, working with musically advanced classes, might suggest that their students "Fill ten seconds with any number of high, short sounds superimposed on three long, low sounds. Create a fluctuating series of dynamics on one sustained pitch. Explore the problems of balancing a series of untuned percussion sounds with some vocal sounds of indefinite pitch in a recurring five-second cycle. Develop three different melodies above ostinato. Treat this melody heterophonically. Compose a rhythmic canon."

These tasks represent modes of behavior that are not traditionally found in the general music class; nevertheless, they are behaviors that are faithful to the discipline of music and to problem-centered learning in the best educational sense.

Preserving the Composition

The final phase in this process involves recording or preserving a composition. In many people's minds a musical composition is virtually synonymous with a written score, but, of course, a composition does not need a score in order to exist. This is an important point because many teachers believe that they cannot encourage children's compositions unless they themselves are capable of handling musical notation fluently. On the other hand, teachers who do possess music reading and writing skills sometimes do irreparable harm by encouraging "paper" compositions based on mechanistic or contrived procedures.

Remember that children learn to write creatively in their own language only after they have had extensive and prolonged aural and verbal experience. Language sounds and meanings are normally well fixed aurally before visual symbols are introduced. The same should be true of music. The teacher's primary task should be to build confidence in working with aural media before using visual notation.

The fourth phase moves from a general visual notation that represents the fundamental characteristics of sound to a more specific notation. Problems have arisen in the past because music educators have attempted to impose a detailed visual system on a generalized aural experience. The tasks associated with this phase should be no less creative than those associated with phases one, two, and three—that is, provided the teacher accepts an elementary, open-ended form of notation. It is illogical to stimulate high-level creativity if later we constrict or stifle it with a fantastically complex set of notational symbols. Simplicity is the essence, therefore, and teachers should encourage children to write notational symbols that match their own creative ideas. For example, "Draw some lines to show the height and depth of these sounds. Which of these symbols might best represent a rough sound? Here are some symbols of different length; think of how many ways you might represent them diagrammatically. Invent some visual symbols that show a range of loud and soft sounds. Write down this phrase using your own notation." One might also work in reverse by having children create sounds suggested by different symbols.

As this phase develops, there will probably be a move toward notational symbols that show definite pitch and precise rhythmic groupings, but this may not be so. Some children will probably be more concerned with process than with product; they will view composition as a unique, one-time thing, as indeed some contemporary composers are doing.

Obviously the tape recorder represents a valid recording device and one whose potential has yet to be fully explored. Its great advantage lies in the ability to capture tonal details that are too complex for even the most comprehensive notational system.

These four phases—sound exploration, sound imagery, sound quality, and sound recording—could provide a framework for building a program in children's composition in the classroom. If teachers are able to approach the subject along these lines, children will be nearer the heart of the musical process.

Orff-Based Improvisation

by Judith Thomas

I have observed many faces of children improvising within musical frameworks: They wear expressions of intense yet relaxed concentration or broadly beaming satisfaction. We have so few reliable ways to measure the unmeasurables at the core of the arts that simple observation becomes an indicator of what is happening inside a child. Children's faces can tell us that they are feeling comfortable, accepting, or delighted at their own ingenuity and musical independence, or are totally absorbed in what they are doing.

I am satisfied to know the merits of improvisation through a child's expression, yet as an educator I know there are other ways to consider its worth. I know that improvisatory experiences are way up on the cognitive ladder—to improvise implies a preliminary knowledge and comprehension of concepts. Then comes the ability to analyze the elements of different concepts. The next level, synthesis, is where improvisation has its home. Here children are finally given the opportunity to design, redesign, reconstruct, rearrange, symbolize, and extend the elements experienced on all previous cog-

nitive levels. They shuffle it all into their own personal shapes: their creations.

Improvisation, particularly as it applies to the Orff-Schulwerk teaching approach, assumes a basic fluency in any given area. It should come *from* somewhere, which assumes preparation, and should flow *to* somewhere, which implies development. Therefore the stage for improvisation must be carefully designed by the teacher, who first provides information and models and who creates tasks involving group and individual experimentation within a nonjudgmental yet analytical atmosphere. This all feeds into a child's improvisational hopper before he or she is asked to synthesize. The richest creations are found where the preliminary ground has been carefully tended.

Improvisatory tasks fall roughly into two categories: "evanescent," where creations are spontaneously realized and instantly gone (song, movement, rhythm, instrumental melody, and so on), or "fixed," where some measure of a statement is held by the memory of the teacher, class, or tape recorder and is later reiterated to become more than a temporal happening. Both types are important. The latter overlaps "creative activities," which often demand a high degree of improvisation. Improvisatory tasks can be approached in groups or individual work, and the structure can be a patterned one, with an established order as the task is passed from one person to the next, or it can be unstructured.

The following improvisation developments and frameworks can be enjoyed with children of all ages.

Judith Thomas is an elementary music specialist for the Upper Nyack Elementary School in Nyack, New York. With Susan A. Katz, she is the coauthor of Teaching Creatively by Working the Word: Language, Music, and Movement. *This article originally appeared in the January 1980* Music Educators Journal.

Sound and Movement

Have students echo combinations from the teacher of "p," "b," "t," "x," "j," and "m" sounds: high, low, fast, slow, sometimes without accompanying movement. Evoke interesting and varied sounds from the children.

Sit in a circle, and, using only hands and arms, pass a motion to the next person as each person makes a sound to accompany it, drawing from earlier experimentation. Evaluate where the circle was most interesting in sound progression and movement variety. A variation of this game is to have students in the circle stand and use the whole body for movement. A leader in the middle can invent a variety of silent movements (using qualities of high, low, fast, slow, sustained) while the group accompanies with vocal sounds, or two leaders in the center can move with a divided circle accompanying with sound. The difficulty of the task is increased because the movers must have awareness of each other. Remind the students that there is silence within music, so there must be occasional stillness. Sustained movement can be assigned to the first leader, with accompanying hand drum sounds (rubbed); the second leader is assigned explosive, expansive movements and given one cymbal to follow. A third leader could be assigned angular movements to be accompanied by wooden instrument sounds.

Have students stand behind a screen that is low enough for them to reach over. Moving with hands only, improvise a "hand play" (like a puppet show without props) with accompanying vocal sounds.

Interpret a shadow dance with sound. Watching a group or individual, improvise a vocal or instrumental sound setting to complement the movements of a shadow dancer moving behind an illuminated screen.

Adding Visuals

Simple visuals can be introduced while using sound and movement concepts. For example, the teacher can invent models of graphics using dots and lines and ask children to find a way to make them "come alive" through sound. Each child can create one graphic and perform it with sound.

Combinations of graphics create music forms: AABA, ABA, and so on. One child's graphic can be used as an ostinato over which sound is improvised by a small group or individual. The entire class could create a group line-and-dot graphic on a large sheet of paper. Expand this graphic by adding a plane of other lines or solid color, indicating another sound source.

To play "Guess-a-Graphic," the class or individual interprets one graphic in sound from a display of a group of pictures. The class decides which is being formed. For "Move-a-Graphic," a similar game, the group or individual improvises a graphic in movement. The child may stand in one place, or may interpret through space while the class guesses which one. Try combining these games. Move and create sound for a graphic. Again, the class tries to identify the target.

Look for Other Designs

Take a nature walk. Find a natural object with interesting markings. Reproduce the markings in a design. Individually find a way to interpret the design (nonpitched percussion, vocal sound, movement, or a combination of these).

Interpret a shirt. Find a piece of clothing or fabric with an interesting pattern, and turn it into a sound and movement improvisation. Use another article of clothing for a contrasting section.

Interpret the room. Consider the outline or texture of objects in the room—for example, the flag, a wastebasket, or a number line. Have the children interpret these through vocal sounds, instruments, or movements. Try adding a vocal ostinato accompaniment.

Interpret a painting created by traditional artists or your own school artists. For a sound interpretation, try using Klee's *Twittering Machine*. For movement, try *Broadway Boogie Woogie* by Mondrian. Create an ersatz Mondrian in paper and tape it to the floor (at least six feet by nine feet in size). Have the children designate vocal and instrumental sounds for the primary colored squares and place isolated tone bells at the ends of the black lines with attendant players. Have someone improvise a dance based on the Mondrian work. When the leader's foot falls on a line corresponding to a tone bell, the person at that line plays; when the leader's feet are on the colors, the prearranged sounds play. For an added challenge, instruct the leader to create a form in his or her improvisation. See if the players can identify the form later.

For other visual sources of improvisation ideas, interpret photographs that have interesting repetitive designs as in sand erosion photos, microscopic cell patterns from a plant, or an aerial view of farmlands. Invent a graphic notation for a new sound. (Try a fire engine sound, a typewriter, a wolf call, a motorcycle, or a cicada). Construct a texture board of various fabrics or paper. Invent movements and sounds for it.

Rotating Rondo

The aim of this activity is to synthesize some basic music elements—pentatonic scales and early rhythmic ostinatos. It assumes previous work on Orff instruments to develop correct mallet grip, good sound production, and so on.

In this "Tinker Tailor" game, the class is seated in a circle around four contrasting instruments (for example, a soprano glockenspiel, an alto metallophone, an alto xylophone, and temple blocks.) The students improvise rhythms, and the teacher writes four of them on the board. On the pitches G and E, four solo voices sing "Tinker, Tailer, Soldier, Sailor" and are joined by the group at "Rich Man, Poor Man, Beggar Man, Thief."

The four soloists move into the center where the instruments are. The teacher calls out the number of a rhythm pattern from the board, which is transferred by the center children to the tonal instruments for a double phrase length (sixteen beats), controlled by the teacher on the bass xylophone. Sixteen more beats are given for free improvisation, with the outside circle clapping the beats. The teacher plays an eight-beat bridge on the recorder, which is the signal for soloists to return to place. The game wordlessly resumes until each person in the circle has had a turn to solo and play in the center. Students in the outside circle can be asked to clap a particular rhythm from the selection on the board.

Singing Hands

The teacher models the first example and improvises a song in C pentatonic using hand signs for *la, sol, mi, re,* and *do* in a slow tempo. The students sing, following the hand signals. Then have a student give the hand signals while other students sing. Evaluate what the class liked about each, or what they found difficult to sing. Discover a way to make the song sound final. The teacher can notate the song as a student uses the hand signals. Longer phrases can be formed by joining compatible fragments.

From Words to Song

The teacher reads words that go with a folk tale called "The Gunny Wolf" (from Bill Martin, Jr., and Peggy Brogan's *Sounds of Mystery,* Holt, Rinehart & Winston, Inc., 1972). The teacher explains that the girl in the story sings nonsense words when she is picking flowers:

> Tray blah tray blah cum qua kimo
> Tray blah tray blah cum qua co

The teacher asks for individuals to volunteer improvised melodies for each phrase, and writes them down as students sing. A simple bourdon accompaniment (such as one alternating between *do* and *sol*) can be improvised by the children.

In a similar game, "The Pentatonic Princess" (see volume 2 of the Orff-Schulwerk American edition of Carl Orff and Gunild Keetman's *Music for Children,* B. Schott's Soehne, distributed by Magnamusic-Baton), students can enjoy creating the movements and sounds for the advancing princes as they arrive by all modes of transportation, hoping to bring the tone of the pentatonic scale they think the princess will like. Students can improvise the recitatives of the princess as she invents pentatonic laments.

Summary

All music has the potential for an improvisatory activity. It might come as an adjunct to a new key. It might take the form of a unit that soothes a hypothetical "savage breast" with lots of movement and rhythmic improvisation in a variety of meters. It might be a complete surprise. At the conclusion of an exploration of hats in a classroom musical presentation of the drama "Hats for Sale", one boy grabbed his favorite purple top hat and a stringless ukulele and improvised a complete and wonderful song about "the music man" who could turn people into anything they wanted to be. The class fell right under his spell and became all kinds of special beings through the magic of his purple hat.

I know of no other approach to music more relevant to the human and musical needs of children than improvisation. These kinds of creative activities keep the teacher in touch with the special abilities and needs of individual children. They set a healthy tone by acknowledging the worth of personal opinions and artistic judgments. Given a positive footing for evaluating improvisation, an artistic bond can be formed in a classroom providing an atmosphere where only the best can happen and where children can reveal their own personal shapes.

Composition as a Teaching Tool

by Jackie Wiggins

Every day in elementary music classrooms, students perform, improvise, listen, and move to music. Few of them actually compose their own music. I have found, however, that composition can be one of the most exciting and rewarding activities for the general music class. Composing can work with general music students for a wealth of reasons: First, children are innately creative; second, composing helps students develop a pride in their own musicality; third, it is a means of teaching and reinforcing musical concepts and a way to address individual abilities and needs, and finally, composition is an excellent tool for evaluation.

I have been using composition with my students for more than fifteen years in six different school districts, and have been especially successful in using it to motivate students to excel in both my classes and in their other musical and academic endeavors. I have developed three lesson-plan approaches: teacher-guided composition, small-group

Jackie Wiggins teaches classroom music at Chestnut Hill Elementary School, Dix Hills (Half Hollow Hills District), New York, and is a doctoral candidate in music education at the University of Illinois at Urbana–Champaign. She is the author of two MENC publications: Composition in the Classroom: A Tool for Teaching *(1990) and* Synthesizers in the Elementary Music Classroom *(1991). This article originally appeared in the April 1989* Music Educators Journal.

composition, and individual free composition. Each technique serves a different purpose in developing the creativity of the students.

I do not teach traditional composition techniques, such as writing balanced, classical phrases or following harmonic rules to create melodies based on chord structures that students have studied previously. My general music students have not been trained to make these harmonic, rhythmic, or melodic decisions, but they have received all the instruction about the elements of music that they need for composing. They can make structural decisions (with the help and guidance of the teacher) that allow them to tap their creativity. Young children make up songs as part of their play. I only take their natural ability one step further and help them produce compositions in the form of written-down improvisations. Students who can notate their own work with either standard notation or their own symbols do so; I help those who cannot.

The quality of the students' compositions is surprisingly high; these children possess greater creativity than I do. My students of all ages view creating music as a natural event in their lives and constantly bring in little slips of paper filled with music or cassette tapes of songs they have written. The resulting selections are a tremendous source of pride for the students and for the school. Children will perform their music for anyone who asks—and even for those who do not. Sometimes the compositions are good enough to be performed on a concert program: In one school concert, students presented both a two-part song written in "soft-rock" style and a composition for four violins.

Different Approaches

You can use various approaches in the classroom to produce student compositions. Students can work together as a class to produce a class song that is usually "published" in a school songbook. My school has a "publishing center," an outgrowth of our language arts program, where student books can be photocopied and bound. This is a convenient resource, but you can also manage publication of student music on your own: It takes only paper, time, and a bit of ingenuity. I have used techniques ranging from simple stapling and mimeographing to producing laminated pages bound together by plastic rings or on hot-glue machines. Performance and in-school publication of students' work is wonderful for boosting school morale. Students eagerly praise and support each other's work, and classroom teachers, administrators, and parents find it very impressive.

In addition to the class approach, you can ask students to work in small groups to produce a specific type of composition so that you can evaluate student comprehension of materials that you have previously taught. Individual free composition should be attempted only by students who have had other composition experiences.

Teacher-Guided Composition

The amount of teacher involvement in teacher-guided class composition will vary with the pedagogical demands of the situation, so you can adapt this technique for use with students ranging from kindergarten to sixth-grade levels. In this method, the children work as a class to compose a song. In the first class session, have the students determine as a group the subject matter and nature of the song. Ask students to volunteer possible topics and then vote on them. Then ask the students to suggest ideas for a poem that will be used as the lyrics of the song. Work out the poem on the chalkboard, editing and rearranging the poem as students come up with more ideas. Take as many students' suggestions as is feasible, guiding the students toward construction of a short poem with a strong rhythmic pulse and rhyme scheme. Sometimes the entire poem will flow spontaneously within a few minutes; in any case, selecting a topic and writing lyrics should take one period.

In the second session, present the class with choices of accompaniment styles that could be used to set the poem. Intentionally suggest some that are appropriate and some that do not match the requirements of the text. Discuss the possibilities and vote on them. The process I use to create the lyrics and melody closely parallels the "process writing techniques" currently being used in many schools. The parallels make it easier for the students to create music, as they have already been introduced to the ideas of forming a main idea, sequencing, classification, and categorizing in their other classrooms. Process writing curricula also introduce students to the concepts of writing by group and individual brainstorming, editing, and revising. Finally, the parallels between the writing curriculum and my composition approach also lend credibility (in the view of most school administrators) to the idea of composing for general music students.

Play an accompaniment in a style selected by the class, choosing a simple and logical chord progression. Chant the text over the accompaniment to establish the rhythm of the melody, and have the class chant with you on subsequent playings. After several times, the class will be able to chant the lyrics alone.

Explain to the class that you want them to sing what they have been chanting. Make it clear that you expect to hear many different melodies simultaneously. Eventually, as you play through the song several times, one melody will emerge. Stronger leaders, or those with better ideas, will lead the others. You must be aware that the voice leading that you use in playing the chords will have a great effect on the outcome; you can use this effect to direct the students unobtrusively toward their best creative work. I generally use a piano to play the chords, but for classes that lack this resource, a skilled music teacher could use a guitar, Autoharp, or other instrument. Once you hear a strong or other instrument. Once you hear a strong melody, stop the class and sing the melody while playing the accompaniment to demonstrate what you hear. Students may not fully realize what their song sounds like until they hear it. If what you sing is what they want, either tape-record it immediately or jot it down quickly on music paper.

By the third session, try to present the class with a notated version of the finished song. Write out the melody, lyrics, and chord symbols, and give each child a copy to keep. At this point you may decide to create an arrangement. Add percussion parts, sound effects, an introduction, interludes, and codas. In my classes, we have recently learned to use electronic instruments; the possibilities are endless.

My classes always perform the finished product for the classroom teacher and for anyone else who will listen. Each year, we publish a songbook and an audiotape of all the songs written by any class or individual in that year. I then edit the tape so that it follows the same order as the songs in the book (using a cassette recorder that has two heads), and the students can take copies of the book and cassette home. They are the most sought-after publications in the school. The students take great pride in their songs, and when they take copies of the songs home and sing them for their parents, I always receive many letters and telephone calls. Community support for our music program has blossomed partly because of this one aspect of the curriculum.

Small-Group Composition

When one uses a conceptual approach to music education, one generally structures lessons around the basic elements of music. I usually introduce an element through a listening lesson and then ask students to manipulate that element in some sort of performance, either composed or improvised. To evaluate the students' comprehension, I often ask students to work in a carefully directed group to create a composition that uses the specific element under discussion. Sometimes we develop these group efforts far enough to publish the results, but

they are usually one-period assignments that I use solely for evaluations.

Students work in groups of four to six for these lessons. Using Orff mallet instruments such as xylophones and percussion instruments, they follow a set of instructions provided on the chalkboard. These instructions must be clear and specific: The more specific the requirements for a lesson, the easier the project will be for the students. I allow about fifteen minutes to complete the project and devote the last ten minutes of the class to group performances of the finished products. The students evaluate the composition in terms of how well each work fulfills the requirements of the assignment. I do not allow artistic judgments, but the good points of a composition may always be recognized by any member of the class. Students are more eager to create music when they know their creativity will not be judged. The nature of these assignments can be varied as

Small-Group Assignment

1. With your group, compose a work in ABA form.
   a. The A music should move in twos.
   b. The B music should move in threes.
   c. Make up a signal or plan for changing from one section to another.
   d. Rehearse your piece.
   e. Be ready by 10:25.

2. Compose a piece that follows this texture chart:

   a. (should be played by a barred instrument)

   b. (should be a single crash)

   c. (should have a steady beat)

   d. (can be any sound)

   e. All four lines should be placed together. The texture should first get thick and then get thin.

   f. Rehearse

   g. Please be ready by 2:20.

Figure 1.

Individual Composition

Individual free composition is the most difficult type of student composition, and it should be attempted only after students have worked as a class and in small groups. It is not necessarily appropriate for all students. In my classes, students begin most of their individual composition in the context of small-group projects. Interested students sometimes ask permission to work alone or at home. The music they create on their own is often some of the best work of the class and a particularly rewarding outcome of my efforts with student composers.

Currently, my fifth and sixth graders, who have been composing with me for three years, rarely write class songs. They have so many ideas as individuals that it has become difficult for them to relinquish their ideas to the group. In last year's songbook, we included twenty-one class songs from grades K–4. My fifth and sixth graders chose to work alone or in small groups and contributed fifty original songs. Three of these were performed at our school concert; several are of such high caliber that I believe they could be published commercially.

Many of my older students write music for their own instruments, so the instrumental teachers help these children work out fingerings and other challenges. The most important aspect of teaching composition at this level is that the students are no longer dependent on the teacher. They are thinking and working like musicians, and they are limited only by their incomplete knowledge of nota-

tion. Most students realize this. They want to be able to read, notate, and play their music. Composing then becomes a tremendous motivating force for learning to read music and for practicing an instrument.

Context and Direction

Composition represents only one aspect of my classroom program. My older students compose during about one-quarter of their time in music class; grades K–3 for about one-sixth. Teaching composition in the general music class requires a different orientation to the curriculum, not different course content. My students view their learning about form, texture, and dynamics as learning about tools they will need to create music. In the minds of the students, the composition element of my curriculum gives credibility to all other elements. Thus, although the finished product is often wonderful, it is the process of composing that is important. The students' skills and musicianship grow with each project. The students learn to weigh the advantages and disadvantages of different stylistic and performance techniques with real maturity.

Students often compose songs that portray their feelings in surprising ways: I have had students create serious, deeply moving songs about the fate of the next generation, hunger, and child abuse. Some have written very funny nonsense and comic songs. All my students have produced compositions that amply demonstrate their developing knowledge of music and of themselves.

Section

To Share:
Performance

In many elementary schools, the music teacher is expected to prepare and present public performances. Most building administrators greatly desire the positive public perception that arises from such occasions. One way of providing public demonstrations of children's music making is through musical plays where an entire class, grade level, or sometimes even an entire school is involved. A second avenue is through concerts by an auditioned or nonselect elementary chorus.

These performance opportunities must be carefully thought out and executed by the elementary music teacher to ensure that music learning occurs during the preparation period. Each of these musical experiences requires a different type of preliminary planning and instruction, and no teacher should begin either type of activity without a thorough understanding of the details involved. The two articles in this section will help teachers understand the preliminary work necessary for a successful children's music performance.

"It's a Hit!"
Planning the Elementary Musical

by Marjorie Nan Webb

The elementary musical can be a worthwhile, integrated learning experience. Students will enjoy helping to create the show, and problems become the basis for lessons in music theory, history, and tone production. A musical provides opportunities for both independent and group participation, as well as an outlet for special talents such as dancing, playing an instrument, costume designing, or painting props.

The key to the successful musical is having an overall plan before the production begins. Communications, budget, music selection, personnel selection, schedules, staging, and costumes should be planned to ensure a trouble-free production. Last-minute adjustments sometimes must be made because of unforeseen circumstances. If proper preparation has been made, however, the last-minute adjustments will be minor.

Eliminating Conflicts

Communications, a vital element through the final rehearsal, should begin a year ahead of production. School administrators need to know about

Marjorie Nan Webb is a research analyst/test counselor at Central Piedmont Community College in Charlotte, North Carolina. This article originally appeared in the October 1986 Music Educators Journal.

your plans so that the production is approved and entered on the school calendar, thus eliminating conflicts. When scheduling, be sure to include rehearsal times and dates when technicians, props, and equipment will be needed. Frustration occurs if some other production ties up these items when they are needed for rehearsals.

Whoever handles the budget needs to know about plans early so that funds can be allocated. Communicate with those who manage the budget, and discuss funds that may be needed, even if they are only minor. People responsible for budgets like to know ahead of time what to expect.

Communications involve many notices and phone calls. Be sure to let homeroom teachers know about plans as soon as possible. They can offer valuable assistance and will need to plan so that students are not on a field trip when a rehearsal is scheduled. Also, talk to people in other departments who may assist with the final production. These could include the staffs of the art department, the physical education department, or those in maintenance and supply. Tell them early what is needed, and be as specific as possible about details. The art department may plan for students to make scenery and props during their regular classes a month or so before the production. The physical education department may teach dance steps during winter classes, even though the knowledge isn't needed until April. Maintenance workers could help build platforms, scenery, or props, and they may need to schedule personnel and equipment to hang banners for the rehearsal and performance.

Communications with the students and parents are also vital. The students need to know how you plan to select the chorus, actors, dancers, and so on. Parents are usually helpful with costumes if they have specific written notices at least a month ahead of time.

Communications should begin early, with reminders and updates scheduled along the way. Changes or additions probably will be made, and all people involved need to know what to expect. Remember the peripheral personnel who may be affected, such as lunchroom workers (who may need to schedule early or late lunch on rehearsal or performance days); secretaries (who need time to type programs); or finance officers (who may need a week or longer to have a check ready for materials or an accompanist).

Many problems never arise if communications are clear, are given in advance, and are received by the right people. The efficient communicator dates, initials, and saves a copy of all written information. Written communications are more reliable and allow everyone to have the same information. Communications from suppliers should be in writing and should be saved to verify information for reporting. After the production is complete, administrators appreciate a brief write-up explaining budget, benefits, and participants.

Creative Budgeting

The budget can be a limiting factor. Purchasing poor or unsuitable music, however, is never economical, no matter how inexpensive it is. A complete musical package with director's copy, rehearsal tape, and twenty-five or thirty student copies costs about a hundred dollars. Other costs include costumes, scenery, props, accompanists, piano tuning, instrumentalists, program, special effects (lighting and so on), and personnel time necessary for a complete production. In spite of all this, it is possible to have a worthwhile musical with little expense by using creative ideas, school equipment, and personnel.

It is not necessary to purchase a commercially packaged musical. Students may write their own, or a teacher may write dialogue encompassing songs and selections available in the music books or music library. The costumes and props may be collected, made in art class, or borrowed with no expense. A classroom teacher may be willing to accompany, and the programs could be typed and copied by the school secretary.

The important consideration in budgeting is to decide how much—if any—money is available and how these funds should best be spent. If good music is purchased, it can be reused in three or four years, or another school in the district might share the expense and use the music the following year. The parent-teacher association might supply funds if the musical is presented for their meeting. The rehearsal tape could be eliminated to conserve funds. Parents, businesses, or organizations might contribute money, supplies, or services.

Choosing the Material

Select the musical well in advance. It is a good idea to examine many items and solicit recommendations from other teachers. If nothing seems suitable, write your own. Sometimes a musical is built around songs from the basic series, or these may be combined with a few traditional songs by writing some dialogue to tie the whole thing together. There are many ways to format the music selection. Whatever is selected, written, or contrived should meet some basic criteria. The following questions should be considered when selecting a musical:

- Is it high-quality music and worth the effort to learn? There are musicals based on a theme (from a famous composer), patriotic songs ("America, the Beautiful"), or collections of folk songs (American or foreign).
- Does it have enough character parts or parts that can be expanded to provide for the number of students who will be in the production (birds, animals, flowers, dancers, warriors, townspeople, and so on)?

- Can it be divided into segments or scenes for easy rehearsal and ease of gathering the groups together?
- Does it offer possibilities for teaching musical concepts?
- Is it within the abilities of the students who will perform it (easy part singing, unison, phrases, vocal range, rhythmic patterns)?
- Are there possibilities for student musicians to perform or provide accompaniment (easy accompaniment for one song; guitar, recorder, or drum parts; Orff-type instrument parts; short vocal solo)?
- Does it require any difficult staging or special effects? Simple is usually best, and children love to imagine.
- What kinds of costumes and props will be needed to be effective? Are these easily available or easy to make?
- Is the designated performance space suitable for the production, or can either be adapted to fit the other?
- Will special effects such as lighting be necessary? If one performance is at night and another is during the day, lighting will be a major consideration.
- Does it require unusual electrical capacity in the designated area? Large spotlights can easily overtax an electrical system.
- Is a rehearsal tape available, or is it needed?
- Are performance requirements stipulated by the publisher (royalty, purchase of a specified number of copies, permission)?

All of these questions apply to each performance, but high-quality music within the abilities of the students must always receive top consideration. It is also important for every student to have a special part in the performance.

The Perils of Casting

Many students will want to have the lead parts. Obviously, some compromise must be made so each child can choose a desirable part. Long and important parts may be double- or triple-cast with one student playing the character in the first sec-tion, another in the middle, and a third in the last section of the musical. Students enjoy this, the audience will understand it if explained, and it gives more students a chance for recognition. With three students playing the lead, rehearsals in small segments are easier, because each classroom will have someone to play that character.

Costuming for students playing the same character may be coordinated, but usually each student wants to choose a costume. Children in the audience, with their well-honed imaginations, usually have no problem following the plot even if the costume of a particular character changes once or twice.

The music educator can list the parts that are available and place a number beside each part indicating how many people could play that role. For example, in Alice in Wonderland, three students could play Alice (part divided), but eight to twelve students might be flowers or cards. On the other hand, in a small class or grade, some adjustment will be necessary so that one student can cover several small parts.

A workable solution to assigning parts is to allow each student to list three choices, from which assignments will be made. It is important to explain beforehand that group-part selections are more available than the lead parts. For example, the student may select the leading part for first choice, but it would be preferable to select another group part (dancer, bird, flower) as choice two or three. By using copies of the same sheet with all parts listed and the number of students who may play those parts, each student selects three choices in order of preference, and signs and returns the sheet. From these selections, the music educator (with help from classroom teachers, if needed) should assign parts, and the students should have an opportunity to choose a part they like.

If proper selection of the musical is made, it is rare a child can't be given one of the selected parts. Should that be the case, the child is contacted, and together the student and educator decide on a suitable part. Parts include stage managers (they move scenery or place props), prompters, program distributors, choreographers, or any job that has to do with the production, as well as speaking and singing parts.

Members of the chorus have the most important parts because they keep the story going. All singing, including numbers designated as solos, can be performed by the chorus. They should be in costumes and may have speaking parts, if necessary. For example, the child who plays Alice may sing with the chorus when not actually part of the main action. Chorus members should be incorporated into the scenes or form a frame around the stage area.

Costuming and Staging

Little costuming is necessary, but most students like to wear something indicating their character. Some students may scoff, but often this is a pretense. The art teacher may help design simple paper hats, cardboard swords, or paper bag garments that the students can work on during class time.

Often a parents' committee will help locate or create suitable costumes. Take advantage of this kind of help. By adding bits of scraps or fur to clothing, clever parents create period styles. Brown, black, or white long-sleeved T-shirts with dark pants or skirts are useful. A sash of wide florist ribbon or aprons can be effective to give a group uniformity. Trim may be glued on white sheets cut to fit for angels; old draperies and bathrobes make kingly robes; towels often serve as turbans; shirts belonging to older sisters, brothers, or parents become tunics; and women's blouses make excellent colonial-type dress shirts for men. Creating costumes or converting other clothing to serve gives the student a chance to use imagination. Let students find, create, or borrow as much as possible. A few parents or grandparents will make beautiful costumes, and some may spend money to rent them.

To designate animals, a band of fabric may be cut to fit across the top of the head and ears or stuffed horns may be attached. Use fake fur in appropriate colors. A creative parent with an interest in crafts may suggest other appropriate methods of constructing needed costumes. A commercial fabric distributor may donate remnants to a class, or damaged fabrics may be available. People who sew may have leftover pieces of material. These may be draped, pinned, or cut with pinking shears to form shirts, shawls, or head coverings.

If each student is asked to supply certain items such as an apron, T-shirt, or hat, be sure to send written notices home several weeks in advance. It is a good idea to include a phone number that parents or guardians can use to get additional information. Often the homeroom teacher will help communicate with the families of students. Some provision should be made for those students who cannot supply even the simplest item.

Staging often involves using a gym, cafeteria, classroom, or multipurpose room as the theater. If there is no scenery available, the art department may be able to help with drawings or paintings on cardboard or paper. Just a few symbolic paintings taped to a wall or post can convey the idea of a castle or outdoor scene. Banners, painted by the students, can be hung from the ceiling to represent a large ballroom.

Folding tables, standing on end, form divisions of space. A small folding screen at one side of the staging arena creates an intimate area. Colored paper stuck to the floor can represent water, boundaries, and so on. Large cardboard furniture boxes have many uses. When painted or decorated, they can become cookie houses, booths, pieces of furniture, boats, or automobiles. Regular school chairs and tables may be draped or covered with paper to form thrones, huts, and the like.

Costuming and staging offer many creative possibilities. Parents, homeroom teachers, special teachers, and maintenance personnel as well as students should be enlisted to develop ideas for simple, effective solutions to the requirements of a particular production.

Tracking the Time

For the music class that meets once a week with a music specialist, about ten to twelve weeks should be allotted for a musical. This could be an extended unit of study or could be divided into two or three units of study encompassing notation, composer, specific style, historical period, and so on. Young children and very short musicals require less time. The following outline shows a possible schedule.

Week 1: Do an overview of the musical with your students. Hear the story, listen to the songs, discuss characters. Encourage students to do research reports on composer, style, and era.

Week 2: Read sections of dialogue. Begin learning themes. Notice musical properties. Teacher explains how characters will be selected.

Week 3: Students receive sheets to select desired part. Study music and learn songs (everybody learns all the music).

Week 4: Students read in sections as the music educator listens carefully and begins to determine those who could carry a major role. Part selection is made so that a classroom can rehearse segments of the musical. Continue study of music.

Week 5: This is the final selection of parts to perform. Continue music study.

Week 6: Use script to begin blocking (stage directions) for general movement. Simulate left and right orientation with designated doors and aisles to conform to the area in which final production will be given.

Week 7: This week includes speaking parts from memory and memorizing music.

Week 8: Block in performance area using small groups (one class, a dance group, one scene). Often a dance group needs to get together in the place of the production. This may require ten or fifteen minutes before school begins or during morning break. A gym in constant use usually has fifteen minutes between classes. These minutes are useful.

Week 9: All props, scenery, dances, and movements should be nearing completion.

Week 10: Plan at least two or three rehearsals in the performance area before the performance. These rehearsals should take no more than twice the time of the musical if small segments have been rehearsed previously. The final rehearsal should be a dress rehearsal with all props.

On With the Show!

A musical can be used as a special performance for parents, other schools and organizations, or simply for a few invited classes. The number of performances will depend on the anticipated audience. Often one performance for parents and a second immediately following for other students will accommodate the audience. Performers usually can give two back-to-back performances before fatigue becomes a problem. Explain exactly where the students are to be for the time between performances and what behavior is expected. Classroom teachers and homeroom parents will be of tremendous help handling large numbers of students.

Musicals will be remembered by students for years. Often an adult remembers the part he or she played in a particular musical. The enthusiasm generated by a production, no matter how simple, is worth the extra effort.

Selecting Music for the Elementary School Chorus

by Janice P. Smith

One of the best results of a strong general music program is a large group of children who love to sing. Once the program is competently staffed, consideration should be given to instituting an elementary school chorus to take advantage of all the youthful talent. Since part singing usually is introduced in the middle grades, most elementary choruses consist of students in grades four, five, and six. A group of approximately sixty to seventy-five students is the largest group that is feasible to instruct. When more students are available, more than one chorus should be created.

Although most elementary music method books mention the idea of forming a chorus (and some give suggestions for organizing, auditioning, and rehearsing such a group), very few suggest a curriculum or discuss how to choose materials. The guidelines that follow will help an elementary choral director select music of lasting value to help make the wisest use of limited funds.

Janice P. Smith is a classroom music specialist at the Asa C. Adams Elementary School in Orono, Maine. This article originally appeared in the April 1987 Music Educators Journal.

Guidelines for Selecting Music

Music selected for any educationally based choral group first should enhance the musical knowledge of the group. Does a particular piece broaden the chorus' stylistic range, or have they sung several works in this style already? Are there changes of dynamics, tempo, or meter that can add to the students' basic musical knowledge? Is it by a composer whose works should be a part of the students' cultural background? Not all of these criteria will be met by all of the selections in a choral repertoire, but the more varied the selections, the greater the repertoire's overall educational value. For each selection chosen for the school music library, the music educator must answer the question "What can I teach my students by using this piece?"

Another consideration is vocal technique or the appropriateness of the piece in the choral curriculum: Will it expand the children's part-singing ability? Is it useful for teaching a certain vowel sound or overcoming a diction problem? Does it require a new skill in phrasing or breath control? Many aspects of choral music education can be taught by using carefully selected musical pieces. A final consideration is programming: Does the particular selection lend itself well to an upcoming program? Although a more extensive discussion of programming for the elementary chorus follows, a selection can be chosen simply because it fits a particular niche in a program.

Screening Compositions

Think about the more practical aspects of selecting choral music. When confronted with a number of possible selections, the choral educator should take the following factors into consideration: First of all, is the work tailored to the physical capabilities of the singers? The overall range of the piece is important. For most elementary choruses the music should not go below the B-flat below middle C or above the top-line F. Examine what vowels are sung above the top-line D—it is very difficult for young people to sing closed vowels at the top of their ranges. (Closed vowels are those sounded with the mouth nearly closed, such as "ee" in *steep*, as opposed to open vowels, such as "ah" in *cot*.)

The tessitura of a selection also is an important consideration. Most of the notes in the piece should fall in the octave from the D above middle C to the top-line D. Look at the melody to see whether there are unusual melodic leaps or extended chromatic passages. Both of these may cause a young chorus difficulty. Likewise, look at the harmony. In her book *Teaching the Elementary School Chorus*, Linda Swears points out that parallel harmonies are not easy for young choirs to sing. She states:

> Children can become confused when the melodic and harmonic line are just a third apart and move in parallel motion. It is difficult for many children to hear the difference between parts written in thirds, and if a child cannot distinguish the difference by ear it is most likely he [or she] will be unable to sing it correctly.[1]

For each selection chosen for the school music library, the music educator must answer the question "What can I teach my students by using this piece?"

When introducing parallel thirds, look for selections that approach the third from a unison. Swears says, "This brief use of contrary motion can help stabilize parts and prevent drifting from one part to another."[2] Parts in contrary motion or songs having dissimilar parts (such as partner songs or pieces that have descants or countermelodies) are easier.

Next, examine the text of the song. Although a considerable amount children's music is available, a great deal of it is inappropriate for elementary school choruses because of the texts. For example, love-song texts are best avoided because children usually find them silly. Look for a text that has value and is communicated in an artistic manner. Make sure the text is not too childish. Conversely, consider whether the chorus will be able to understand and convey the meaning of the words to an audience. Finally, does the musical setting effectively enhance the meaning of the lyrics?

The choral educator should look for interesting accompaniments to the piece. Try to avoid accompaniments that double the voices or overshadow the chorus. Whether the accompaniment is simply piano or is a combination of instruments, it should complement the composition and should not compete with the chorus for the audience's attention.

Next to be considered are programming possibilities. Is the selection reusable? Is it appropriate for different types of performances and audiences? Music that can be used only once every six or so years may not be the most efficient use of funds.

Last of all, the choral director should form an aesthetic judgment of the piece. Does it have the discernible quality? Is it worth the time it will take to prepare? Does the selection have a message to communicate? Will the chorus members like the selection immediately, or will they grow to like it? Will it challenge the director and provide satisfaction? If the answer is "yes" to these few questions, that may be reason enough to add the selection to the choral library.

Program Structure

When planning either one program or an entire year of programs, you will find that many of the considerations are the same as for other school choral groups. The director must consider the audience for whom the chorus will perform. A public evening performance should contain selections with a higher degree of sophistication than that found in pieces done at an in-school concert. A performance for the choral director's peers calls for yet another type of programming. Therefore, the audience is an important consideration when selecting music for a program.

Special attention always should be given to the opening number on a program because it sets the tone for the rest of the performance. The selection should be lively, easy for the chorus, and entertaining for the audience. If possible, the chorus should take their positions while singing this selection so that the audience does not have to sit and wait for them to file into position.

The prudent choral educator will put the more difficult selections near the beginning of the program, though not at the very beginning. These selections probably will tire young singers and are better sung while the performers are at their freshest. The lighter, easier selections can be done during the second half of the program.

Obviously, the program should have variety. The audience enjoys pieces that vary in tempo and mood. The choral director should try to follow a lively, crisp selection with a slower, lyrical one. Programming two slow selections in a row can be boring to the audience and enervating to the performers. In the same vein, the director should attempt to provide clear contrasts in dynamics, not only within a given composition but also between selections on the program. Differences in rhythmic intensity also will add to the feeling of tension and release.

A Diverse Performance

An interesting program also should include some variations in the type of accompaniment. At least one selection should be performed a cappella, for even the most elementary-level choruses need to experience this type of sound. Many beautiful rounds can be performed this way. Thought should be given to using classroom instruments, record-ers, flutes, or percussion to enhance the performance. Chorus members often perform on other instruments and welcome the opportunity to display their talents.

Another means of providing variety is to vary the size of the performing group. A director can form a small group of performers who learn a more difficult work, have the boys sing alone, or include solos either within a composition or as a separate selection. Occasionally the choral director should program a selection involving audience participation. Many people who attend choral concerts are former chorus members who would enjoy the chance for some personal music making in a nonthreatening environment. A variation of this is to have former chorus members who are in the audience join the onstage chorus to perform a traditional selection.

Finally, the choral director should consider ending the program with something familiar. This will be easier for the singers and will leave the audience with a sense of participation by recognition. Patriotic selections, show tunes, or spirituals are good choices for concluding a program.

Success through Unity

In spite of the need for variety in programming, there also must be a sense of unity. This can be achieved both by carefully balancing the contrasts and by using a theme such as "Winter Holiday," "Christmas Around the World," or "Songs of Freedom." Singing an unrelated series of songs may teach a chorus a variety of skills, but it will not provide as effective and satisfying a performance as will a program with a theme. This is not to say that the theme should dictate what materials the chorus members learn, for presumably not everything they sing will be practiced to the degree necessary for performance. The choral director should, however, give consideration to how a given selection will fit into a program and then purchase music accordingly.

Unity in a program also can be provided by performing the selections in chronological order; however, the selections must be drawn from various time periods. The *Juilliard Repertory Library*

(Canyon Press, Cincinnati) is an excellent resource for elementary school choral directors wishing to try this approach. Compositions in a wide variety of styles, composers, and levels of difficulty are included in this collection.

Take Time to Prepare

One final consideration in selecting music for an elementary chorus is the quality of the educational experience for the group. Far more learning will take place if the director uses a few carefully chosen, well-prepared selections over the course of a year than if a great many pieces are constantly being prepared but never reach performance level. In a truly worthwhile selection, there always are new depths to be probed. (The chorus' repertoire can be expanded over time by reusing pieces from a previous year, since only the new students will have to learn the parts. This should not be done to excess, however. One or two familiar selections for every four to six new selections is a reasonable separation.

Thoughtful selection of music for the elementary chorus with an eye for its educational and performance value is time well spent by the choral director. Limited financial resources will be used wisely, rehearsal time will be spent on music of value, and performances will be rewarding for the performers, the audiences, and the conductor.

Notes

1. Linda Swears, *Teaching the Elementary School Chorus* (West Nyack, NY: Parker Publishing, 1985), 104.

2. Swears, 164.

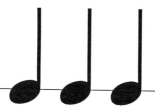

Section

5

To Be Most Effective:
Partnership

The final article in this collection deals with a most important but often undiscussed aspect of elementary music teaching. One can have the highest degree of musicianship and a superb undergraduate grade point average and still be a less than effective music teacher if the influence of one's teaching peers is neglected.

Those who are devoted to their subject yet wish to be known as cooperative members of the school faculty must walk a very fine line. Music teachers may be asked to integrate their subject with other curricula and to provide their teaching peers with "user-friendly" materials. Some classroom teachers, however, may view music as less than valuable or only as an addition that can make learning other subjects more interesting. Music teachers who are aware of these outlooks may want to adopt the campaign suggested in the following article and build a "support network" with their peers.

Classroom Teachers: Elementary to Music Education

by Sue A. Malin

All too often, elementary music teachers find themselves in situations with their elementary classroom peers that are less than encouraging. In fact, these situations can be downright discouraging. Do such events happen to you? Read the following scenarios, and see if you recognize yourself.

Scenario 1

Ms. Smith, a traveling music teacher, was ready for another day of eleven elementary music classes. She had carefully planned and packed her cart for the five classes that she would teach before lunch. Confident and in high spirits, she wheeled her cart into the first class. Before she began to teach, the classroom teacher rose to depart. As he did so, he said to the children, "Sing pretty," and to Ms. Smith, "It must be great to be a music teacher and have fun all day."

When the class ended, Ms. Smith repacked the cart and moved to the next class. When she entered, she saw the students' heads buried in their textbooks. The classroom teacher scowled at the

Sue A. Malin is an associate professor of music at Lock Haven University, Lock Haven, Pennsylvania. This article originally appeared in the November 1988 Music Educators Journal.

interruption, looked at the clock, and said, "Is it time for music already? We're right in the middle of our math lesson! Well, we'll have to stop. Get out your music books!" After much clanging of desk lids and paper shuffling, Ms. Smith was able to start the lesson, but it took too much time to motivate the students. By the time she had drawn them into the lesson, it was time for her to leave.

Scenario 2

Mr. Jones is the general music teacher for two elementary schools and one middle school. Along with his general music duties, he is responsible for teaching two elementary school choirs and a woodwind class at the middle school. On this particular morning, he stopped at the teacher's lounge for coffee before classes. As he entered, one teacher was saying, "I don't think specialists should be paid the same as classroom teachers. After all, they only teach one subject."

Scenario 3

Ms. Brown is an elementary music teacher who has her own music rooms in two schools. On this same morning, she stopped to talk with the classroom teacher before starting music class. Ms. Brown asked the teacher if she would play a recording of a song throughout the week so that the children would be better prepared for a program. The classroom teacher replied, "No, I don't have time. By the way, I am keeping Bobby out of music this week. He has not been doing his work."

The Problem

Do these situations seem farfetched, or have they happened to you? These scenes were actual events. In each case, something was wrong. In Scenario 1, the classroom teacher gave the students the impression that they should not take music seriously. He sees the music teacher as a provider of fun, and perhaps even as a baby-sitter. The second classroom teacher in Scenario 1 shows her annoyance with angry words. She perceives music as an interruption of a more "important" subject. The teacher in the lounge in Scenario 2 does not consider Mr. Jones a professional. Finally, in Scenario 3, fellow teachers do not consider Ms. Brown a partner in teaching and do not consult her when making decisions concerning student behavior.

These negative attitudes undermine the professional nature of an elementary music program. Articles written about public relations with administrators, school board members, parents, and students focus on changing or influencing attitudes. More needs to be written about the music educator's need for public relations with the elementary classroom teacher. Should this be an additional responsibility for already overloaded music teachers? There are several sources the music teacher can refer to that demonstrate convincingly that it should.

All music educators know the importance of achieving and maintaining positive attitudes among their students. Shirley Strom Mullins stated that, in a student, a positive attitude is the most important factor that affects learning.[1] Who is the most consistent influence on the student's attitude day after day? Of course, it is the classroom teacher. Research has shown that teacher approval increases students' on-task behavior.[2] The classroom teacher who shows enthusiasm for music activities can positively influence students' attitudes and behavior toward music. Why, then, do so many music teachers ignore this influential power that classroom teachers wield?

It is not always easy to get along with classroom teachers; each individual has a unique personality and teaching style. The elementary music teacher often sees this teaching style reflected in the distinct personality of each class. The classroom teacher's influence does not stop with the students, however. In some cases, classroom teachers have direct contact with the principal every day. The principal knows what is happening by listening to the teachers talk about instructional and curricular concerns, by listening to the opinions of the specialists, and by hearing reports from various parents. Classroom teachers have frequent contact with parents. Often, parents talk to classroom teachers first about activities in the specialists' classes. Not only do classroom teachers see the same students each day, but they also retain contact with former students in the hallway, at recess, at lunch, and at the bus. As a result, the influence of the classroom teacher is apparent in every aspect of school life.

When you begin to realize how visible classroom teachers are, you start to understand that you must have them on your side. You have to change unfavorable attitudes into positive, supportive ones for music, since these attitudes are in evidence even when you are not present.

Solving the Problem

Devising a campaign to build favorable attitudes toward an elementary music program is a deliberate act.[3] It takes planning and conviction on the part of the music teacher for it to work. A 1958 MENC publication, *The Music Teacher and Public Relations*, provided advice for the elementary music teacher that is still helpful today. MENC recommended following the "inside-out concept" of public relations. This concept stresses that you should make every effort to improve your interaction with each person you see on a daily basis. Music teachers also need to understand and participate in discussions with the entire faculty about general concerns.

All these recommendations seem to be common sense. Indeed, you may be saying, "I know all this." But because the music specialist has a busy schedule and works daily with several hundred students, dozens of teachers, and several administrators, it is easy to see how public relations can be neglected. It is extremely important that elementary music teachers take time to reevaluate public relations in their schools. At the very least, the appearance and presence of the music teacher has an effect on the attitude others have toward the music program.[4] As *The Music Teacher and Public Relations* reminds us, a music specialist is judged first as a person and second as a musician.

So, with eleven classes a day and dozens of classroom teachers with whom to cope, how do you build positive attitudes while struggling to maintain your own? The following suggestions may help you devise a plan to fit your particular situation:

1. *Become actively interested in your classroom colleagues.* Try the "FORM" recipe for talking to people.[5] This process will help you communicate with even the most negative teacher. The "F" stands for "family." Most classroom teachers consider their students to be their "kids." Talk to the teachers about their "family," and you will glean a wealth of information that will help you be more effective with the students. The "O" is for "occupation." Engage teachers in conversations about their careers, goals, and techniques. You can learn effective class management techniques from getting teachers to talk about what they do. "R" stands for "recreation." Ask teachers what their favorite music is or if they have ever played an instrument. You will probably hear many delightful stories about high school band and choral experiences. Finally, "M" stands for "message." At this point, you can talk about the music program goals or how the particular teacher or grade level fits into the music program.

When you try this method, you will find that people love to talk about themselves. They will know that you are interested in them as fellow educators and, in turn, will give you and your program more support. The other benefit of using the "FORM" method is that you will become a bigger part of the educational fabric of the school. The information and insight you gain from the teachers will help you improve your teaching of their classes. You will also find that there are many teachers who have the same zest for their work as you do, and they are eager to talk about it. If you use this method, coffee breaks will no longer be gripe sessions but rather pleasant times for exchanging ideas. Appointments with difficult colleagues will quickly become give-and-take professional sessions.

2. *Avoid complaining about the students.* Since classroom teachers see their students as "their kids," they may be sensitive to any complaints about behavior. Be diplomatic, and accentuate the positive.

3. *Use "Happygrams."* These are positive reports sent to teachers, classes, or parents. Whenever a class does an outstanding job, send a "Happygram" to the classroom teacher. It will be posted proudly for all to see, and it can produce more positive behaviors and attitudes toward music.

4. *Invite classroom teachers to stay in the room as you teach music, or welcome them in your classroom.* Set the date in advance so the teacher can keep that time free. Students get excited at the possibility of having their teacher hear their songs, see them play instruments, or watch them dance. Many times the children want their teacher to join in. This is an excellent way to enhance your curriculum.

5. *Publish a monthly newsletter that includes a calendar of the events in which you are involved.* Many teachers forget that they share you with another school. The calendar will serve both as reminder so they can avoid surprises in schedule changes and as a demonstration of how active you are.

6. *Send out written notices if your schedule needs to change.* Make sure to do this several weeks in advance of the changed date.

7. *Realize that when you change your schedule, you will change the classroom teacher's schedule as well.* Thank the teacher with a handwritten note of appreciation. If the schedule change affects several of the teachers, thank them by bringing treats to the teacher's lounge. They can lift the spirits of tired teachers, make friends, and win support. Next time you need cooperation, you will find it much easier to solicit.

8. *Make every effort to visit classrooms to see displays or to observe daily events.* One minute spent looking at the children's work shows both the teacher and the students that you care about them and their school. If possible, visit classrooms during special events like holiday parties. Ask the teacher first; you will be surprised at how welcome you will be.

9. *Attend school meetings, open houses, and parent-teacher meetings whenever possible.*

10. *Give teachers a list of the music materials you have available for use in the elementary classroom.* Never assume that the teachers know what is available in the library or the music room. Make them aware that you are available to sign out materials, lend instruments, or help them in other ways as necessary.

11. *Realize that all teachers are busy; do not complain about your work load.* Negative behavior will always be remembered.

12. *If you travel between schools, resist the urge to talk about other schools' problems and personalities.* Every school is different, and you will have your preferences, but they are best kept to yourself.

13. *If a teacher forgets to send a class to music, go get the students.* You will be proving your interest in your program. The teacher will be thankful that you remembered, and so will the children.

Build a Network

You must realize that successful public relations with classroom teachers are an essential element for the implementation and growth of the music program. If you are a competent music educator and can build a support network among the elementary classroom teachers, your music program will succeed and thrive.

If the teachers in the opening scenarios learn to implement these suggestions successfully, they might hear responses such the following:

To Ms. Smith: "Is it music time already? Great! Put your math away and get ready for a fine music class."

To Mr. Jones in the lounge: "I am glad that you sent us your schedule. It'll help me plan. I had no idea that you taught all of those grades, plus choir and band instruments, too! You certainly teach more than I thought."

To Ms. Brown: "I'd be glad to play the record for the students this week. By the way, Bobby has been neglecting his work; please observe his behavior today, and we will check with each other later."

What a difference! Is this really fiction? Not at all. Classroom teachers can become supporters of your program; respect them and they will respect you.

Notes

1. Shirley Strom Mullins, "Attitude," *The Instrumentalist* 39, no. 5, 1984, 16.

2. Clifford K. Madsen and Robert A. Duke, "Perception of Approval/Disapproval in Music Education, *Bulletin of the Council for Research in Music Education*, no. 85, 1985, 119-30.

3. Oscar W. Knade, Jr., "Building Support for Music Education," *Pennsylvania Music Educators News* 49, no. 2, January 1985, 14-15.

4. Margaret Dee Merrion, "Guidelines on Classroom Management for Beginning Music Educators," Music Educators Journal 66, no. 6, February 1980, 47-49.

5. Dan Robinson, *Contacting and Inviting Techniques* (Audiocassette). Los Angeles International Executive Department, no. 104, 1985.

Other Best of *MEJ* Books

Creativity in the Music Classroom: The Best of *MEJ*
This book contains sixteen classic *MEJ* articles that give philosophical support for creativity in the music classroom, define creativity, investigate the place of creativity in the curriculum, and discuss the incorporation of creativity in the classroom through the use of action studies and ideas. Edited by Donald L. Hamann. 1991. 120 pp. Stock #1610.

The Music Educator and Community Music: The Best of *MEJ*
The nineteen articles in this collection offer a retrospective of the importance of school and community music during America's past and present. Edited by Michael L. Mark. 1992. 104 pp. Stock #1612.

Other Related MENC Materials

Teaching General Music: A Course of Study
This work offers music teachers a model for developing a strong program of instruction for teaching courses in general music. The course covers all levels from preschool to high school; outlines aspects of the curriculum including performing/reading, creating, listening/describing, and valuing; and offers objectives and procedures within each topic. Developed by the MENC Task Force on General Music Course of Study. 1991. 40 pp. Stock #1602.

Choral Music for Children
This annotated list of works composed or arranged for the unchanged treble voice mentions music from a wide variety of musical styles; describes the music's characteristic qualities, form, style, and value for education; provides tips for teaching and presentation; and presents cross-references by composer, title, voicing, and level of difficulty. Edited by Doreen Rao. 1990. 176 pp. Stock #1502.

Promising Practices: High School General Music
The ten contributors to this collection describe innovative and thought-provoking programs to aid music educators in developing effective general music courses. The work includes sample lesson plans and presents practical considerations involved in managing each program examined. Edited by Mary Palmer. 1989. 112 pp. Stock #1499.

For more information about these and other MENC publications, write:

MENC Publications Sales
1902 Association Drive
Reston, VA 22091-1597

For fast service, credit-card holders may call
1-800-828-0229, Monday–Friday, 8:00 A.M.–4:00 P.M. EST.